THE TRIPLE C WRITING SYSTEM · FOR SUCCESS!

Mastering Short-Response Writing:
Claim It!
Cite It!
Cement It!

ALAN SITOMER

SCHOLASTIC

Dedication

This work is dedicated to Lois Bridges, an indefatigable champion of teachers and students, who deserves a statue built in her honor for the great work she has done—and continues to do—in the world of literacy instruction.

Acknowledgments

Throwin' a big SHOUT OUT to the entire Scholastic Team (particularly Lois Bridges, Danny Miller, Sarah Longhi, Ray Coutu, Sarah Morrow, and Suzanne Akceylan) for all your brains, energy, talent, tolerance of my shenanigans, and heart. Love you guys!

. . . .

Scholastic is not responsible for the content of third-party websites and does not endorse any site or imply that the information on the site is error-free, correct, accurate, or reliable.

Photo on page 41 © Pete Souza/The White House via Flickr.

Cover Designer: Jordan Wyss
Acquiring Editor: Lois Bridges
Copy/Production Editor: Danny Miller
Interior Designer: Sarah Morrow

CONTENTS

Before You Read

I began my writing career under ideal conditions: as an overworked, under-resourced, chronically exhausted inner-city classroom teacher simply seeking to write something—*anything*—that my reluctant readers would read.

Oh, did I say ideal? I meant *INSANE*!

Of course, the passion to reach my kids (because I knew in my bones they were reachable despite the dismal data) fueled my inner fire but it also threw my schedule into a tizzy. On school nights I'd write from 9:00 p.m. to midnight knowing I needed to rise at 5:00 a.m. to be at school early enough to have some calm-before-the-storm time in my classroom (alone) so I could launch my school day on a positive, well-organized note. Saturdays became novel-writing days, every other Sunday, too, and with the help of lots of coffee, I broke through.

I've now written 20 books. Without a doubt, the biggest benefit of becoming a professional writer is that it turned me into a much better teacher of writing. Passion may have ignited the desire for me to write books that would resonate with young readers but, as all writers learn, passion is not enough. Passion runs out of gas. Writers need more than zeal, enthusiasm, and desire; writers need skills.

Thus this book, *Mastering Short-Response Writing: Claim It! Cite It! Cement It!* I've designed it to be a common sense tool for common sense instruction that enables educators to reap highly uncommon—yet highly attainable—results.

We can build strong student writers with skills that transfer across the disciplines—as well as beyond the classroom walls—which will last our kids a lifetime. And to do so will open a world of possible.

Good luck,

Alan Sitomer

"Writing might be magical, but it's not magic. It's a process, a rational series of decisions and steps that every writer makes and takes, no matter what the length, the deadline, even the genre."

—DONALD MURRAY
PULITZER PRIZE-WINNING JOURNALIST
AND WRITING TEACHER

Simplicity Leads to Success

Mastering Short-Response Writing: Claim It! Cite It! Cement It! is all about simplicity. The instructional model that focuses on the Triple Cs is simple. The student writing tasks are simple. The escalation of cognitive demands are simple.

Why? Because when it comes to building rock-solid short-response writers, simplicity leads to success.

However, do not mistake simplicity for inelegance or nonrigor. By the time your students have progressed through the Triple Cs (Claim it! Cite It! Cement It!), you'll discover that by concentrating on simplicity you have opened a door to both complexity and creativity. Student writing will flourish but it will do so based on nothing more opulent than sound fundamentals.

These pages are dedicated to one art: teaching young writers how to compose an expository or argumentative short response that:

1. Makes a claim. CLAIM IT!

2. Supports the claim with evidence. CITE IT!

3. Connects the evidence to the claim to create a rock-solid response. CEMENT IT!

By proceeding one step at a time with an emphasis on the brass tacks, you'll soon bear witness to students who compose intelligent, multidimensional short responses that are clear, concise, cogent, and (practically) free of mechanical and/or grammatical errors.

This is Tortoise and the Hare writing instruction whereby we move at a pace that is developmentally appropriate for young writers. Yes, we want kids to fashion articulate assertions, offer compelling proofs, use vibrant language, ascend the heights of Bloom's Taxonomy while incorporating Aristotlean reasoning, and do it all while wielding semicolons like Zorro wields a whetted blade. However, the only way to arrive at this point is by proceeding strategically.

Through the Triple Cs: Claim It! Cite It! Cement It!, students not only learn the material, but the learning sticks!

Once upon a time, Ernest Hemingway famously pointed to the K-I-S-S principle when it came to producing high-quality writing: Keep It Simple, Stupid. We're definitely believers that Keeping It Simple is the surest path to attaining success. I've seen it with my own students and I have great confidence these ideas will allow you to reap significant and lasting gains with yours.

Mastering Short-Response Writing: Claim It! Cite It! Cement It! is a research-based approach to writing instruction that builds confident, capable short-response writers who own the ability to compose argumentative and expository short responses that evidence accomplished, impressive skills.

Time to sharpen our proverbial pencils . . . here we go!

CHAPTER 1

Why Short Response?

Sarah, a brand new first-year teacher who was struggling with her writing instruction, came to me for help but, much to her surprise, I told her I didn't want to see her student essays. More important, I felt, was to begin with the actual assignment. She dug into her teaching bag and pulled out the following task after explaining that it was a baseline measurement district writing assessment she'd been mandated to give her kids:

Assignment

Write a narrative essay relating your own experiences to the points the author makes in the passage. Perhaps you or someone in your family has accumulated too much; if this has not been your experience, picture a time when it might be. Using the information

> from the passage, follow your life as you go through phases of accumulation and clearing out. Develop your narrative using effective technique, well-chosen details, and well-structured event sequences, and be sure to include references to the passage in your response.

This prompt struck me as a head scratcher—for about a thousand reasons. Yet the assignment proved illuminating. One of the foremost problems we have when it comes to teaching students how to write well is self-evident: we are incessantly asking students to write long, multiparagraph essays when it is clear that our students do not have the skills necessary to compose well-written short responses.

Of course Sarah's students bombed. With a prompt like the one above—knowing her kids' abilities as well as she did prior to giving them the assignment—why would anyone expect anything different?

This truth may come off as uncomfortable to acknowledge but the real problem is not the low writing skills of our kids; the real problem belongs to the well-meaning but misguided educators who are unintentionally setting our students up for failure.

No one asks a neophyte pilot to reenter Earth's orbit from the cockpit of a rocketship when you know they don't have the skills to fly a crop duster. No one asks a neophyte chef to prepare a five-course gourmet meal when they know the cook doesn't have the skills to make toast. Asking a neophyte writer to pen a multiparagraph, nuanced, and complex essay when you know they do not have the skills to compose a simple, single, sure-footed paragraph doesn't make sense and short-circuits our primary goal—improving our students' writing skills.

We are asking students to write long, multiparagraph essays when it is clear that many of our students do not have the skills necessary to compose well-written short responses.

Yep, the emperor has no clothes. Our poorly conceived instructional paradigm for teaching writing needs to be challenged—and reimagined. This is clear.

But how?

Like eating an elephant, it's a matter that needs to be digested one bite at a time. What follows are three initial "chewing points" to consider before moving forward.

CHEWING POINT 1: FORGET THE "SHOULDS"

To tackle this challenge smartly, we must first forget the "shoulds." "They already should know how to capitalize a proper noun" or "They already should know how to use an apostrophe" or "They already should know how to develop a richly expressed narrative that demonstrates an ability to structure event sequences in a logical and cohesive order." These beliefs about what "ought" to be are hampering our aims.

We can squawk all we want in the lunch room about what our students "should" be able to do, but effective writing instructors understand that the only way to improve performance begins with accepting that kids are where they are and that we, as teachers, need to meet them where they are, and build their abilities upward from there. There is no "should"; there is only what is. (Pretty zen, huh?) The sooner the "should" sentiment is kicked to the curb, the sooner we will be able to set to the task of building competent, confident, capable writers.

CHEWING POINT 2: QUIT PRETENDING WE DON'T ALREADY KNOW WHAT WE ALREADY KNOW

Sarah did not need this writing assignment to tell her that her students were not able to meet the demands of this writing assignment. And neither did her district. Nor did her principal, her superintendent, or the Secretary of Education for the United States of America.

It certainly can't come as a gigantic surprise for anyone in education to know that the lion's share of our nation's kids do not write well. We own reams of data, test scores, pie charts, graphs, and internationally benchmarked assessments that already make it abundantly clear that American kids, for the most part, well . . . I want to put this delicately . . . write rotten.

CHEWING POINT 3: WE MUST OWN IT: MOST OF OUR KIDS WRITE ROTTEN

Let's take a moment to really let it soak it in: by almost any measure, by and large, American students are lousy writers.

Ouch. It stings. Badly.

Okay, now that we've faced the truth, let's take a moment to recognize that we're the ones who charted the writing waters we're currently sailing and if we continue to do what we are doing, we'll get what we've consistently been getting over the past few decades.

It's time to break the cycle of dysfunctional writing instruction.

There's a phrase often attributed to Einstein: "The definition of insanity is doing the same thing over and over and expecting different results." So what are we doing (and how do we need to change)? It turns out our solutions are not hidden away in a secret crypt protected by ghouls and werewolves and, most terrifying of all, Justin Bieber.

Hallelujah! Hope exists.

The Common Sense Answer About Effective Writing Instruction
(About Which There Is Little to No Dispute)

Since he's smart enough to quote twice in one chapter, let's bounce back to Einstein who reportedly said, "Everything should be made as simple as possible, but not simpler." So, what's the simplest path to making sure our students can competently compose long, thoughtful pieces of text?

The answer is making sure they can competently compose short, thoughtful pieces of text. Making sure that students have mastered short-response writing is critical to their college and career readiness. This really is the silver bullet to successful writing instruction, and skipping this critical step in the process of teaching students how to write well is more than just silly; it's educational malpractice.

In no uncertain way, we are currently handicapping our young writers by not ensuring foundational skills are firmly in place before they matriculate to higher grades. Students who haven't nailed down the fundamentals of writing rock-solid short responses in their early years will almost always see their deficiencies boomerang and come back to bite them later on down the line.

This phenomenon is an educational truism that holds water across all disciplines, too. For example, in math, a student who hasn't mastered basic math facts and multiplication tables will almost always run into unsurpassable problems once they hit geometry. In science, a student who doesn't have a strong understanding of the basic structures of cells is going to become roadkill in AP Biology. A music student who can't play *Chopsticks* on the piano will never be able to play Beethoven's 5th *Sonata*. A thousand examples could be cited. We learn how to hike hills before we hike Everest. That's just the way human beings are built. Writing instruction cannot violate this principle.

Of course, I am not alone in my thinking. As Sarah Tantillo, author of *The Literacy Cookbook* (Jossey Bass, 2012) points out, "If we keep expecting students who can't construct decent sentences to magically produce coherent essays, we'll remain a nation of lousy writers forever." Natalie Wexler, editor of the blog Greater Greater Education, said the following in *The Washington Post*: "Many students have no idea how to write a paragraph that hangs together, let alone a coherent five-paragraph essay. They don't understand how to draw a connection between a claim and a piece of evidence, a basic necessity in constructing a logical argument. These aren't just writing skills. These are thinking skills of the type the students will need to succeed in college, on the job or even just to dispute a charge on a credit card bill—and to knowledgeably exercise their right to vote."

Three cheers, Ms. Wexler! Next time you are in Los Angeles, I'd like to buy you a soy, chai, half-caf, no sugar, organic, yerba mate latte.

Put quite simply, multiparagraph essays are composed one paragraph at a time. Paragraphs are composed one sentence at a time. If a student is struggling to compose single sentences and the instructor is demanding long, extended essays, is it really the kid's fault when the whole enterprise collapses under its own ill-considered weight?

A better instructional schema will produce tangible, measurable, sustainable growth. Kids must properly learn how to build rock-solid short responses. Crawl before you walk, walk before you run . . . who doesn't get this?

Newsflash! We Live in a Short-Response World

Teaching students how to craft rock-solid short responses is not merely a bridge to teaching multiparagraph essay writing; teaching students how to write rock-solid short responses is a highly valuable skill in and of itself.

Like it or not, we now live in a short-response world.

From emails to cross-curricular writing tasks to social media posts to standardized tests and assessments across the disciplines, short response rules the day. Attention spans are down, information overload is up, and the people who know how to be pointed, concise, and cogent with brisk, clean, mechanically sound writing possess a valuable skill that will serve them well in and out of school for the rest of their lives.

BUT IT'S EASY TO WRITE A SHORT RESPONSE. AFTER ALL, THEY'RE "SHORT," RIGHT?

Not at all. In fact, and this may strike some as counterintuitive (because in school we often conflate the length of an assignment with the rigor of the task), but lots of intelligent people have noted that writing a short response is much more challenging than writing a long one.

Perhaps French philosopher Blaise Pascal said it best. (If he said it at all—some say it was Abraham Lincoln or Mark Twain. Either way, the point is still the same.)

> "I would have written a shorter letter, but I did not have the time."
>
> —BLAISE PASCAL

CHAPTER 2

Explicit Instruction:

What It Is, Why It's Effective

Let's pause for a few definitions so we're all on the same page. Implicit learning is essentially a passive process where students acquire knowledge through exposure to models. In his book *Principles of Language Learning and Teaching* (2005), Douglass Brown defines implicit learning as "learning without conscious attention or awareness." Simply put, students' skills evolve through exploration and trial and error as they come to discover "right" answers through self-reflection and contemplative deduction.

Explicit instruction, on the other hand, is a systematic method of teaching that emphasizes small steps that are unambiguously explained and thoughtfully modeled. It's a direct approach to education where students are overtly and expressly guided.

In their book *Explicit Instruction: Effective and Efficient Teaching*, Anita Archer and Charles Hughes describe it like this:

> Explicit instruction is characterized by a series of supports or scaffolds, whereby students are guided through the learning process with clear statements about the purpose and rationale for learning the new skill, clear explanations and demonstrations of the instructional target, and supported practice with feedback until independent mastery has been achieved. (Archer and Hughes, 2010)

Both camps have their research base; both camps have their benefits and limitations as to why their preferred approaches are an epistemologically sound choice.

No need to get into those weeds. In fact, I am not even sure that I know what the word *epistemological* means. What I do know is that I really like the fact that explicit instruction operates on a research-based model for building skills that is inclusive of all learners and has proven to be a particularly effective strategy to use with low-performing students.

Perhaps that's why I am so swayed toward using it—most of our student writers are low performers. Counting on them to absorb or deduce or infer or intuit how to best frame a well-written response by simply reading enough models and taking enough stabs at writing one is a strategy that, to my way of thinking, is not enough. It's somewhat akin to saying that if students simply watch enough television, they'll one day learn how to become excellent television actors.

It doesn't quite work that way.

On the other hand, unambiguously explaining to student writers what to do, clearly modeling for them how to do it, and smartly guiding them through hands-on practice so that they can gain mastery over each individual area of focus strikes me as a cogent approach.

And I like cogency. It epistemologically resonates, if you know what I mean.

Explicit instruction also allows writing instructors to incorporate Fisher and Frey's Gradual Release of Responsibility Model (based on the original Pearson, Gallagher, 1986 model) into their teaching practice.

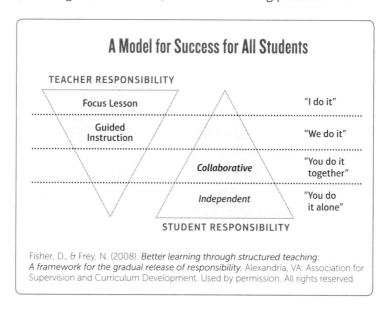

A Model for Success for All Students

TEACHER RESPONSIBILITY

Focus Lesson	"I do it"
Guided Instruction	"We do it"
Collaborative	"You do it together"
Independent	"You do it alone"

STUDENT RESPONSIBILITY

Fisher, D., & Frey, N. (2008). *Better learning through structured teaching: A framework for the gradual release of responsibility.* Alexandria, VA: Association for Supervision and Curriculum Development. Used by permission. All rights reserved.

I like the Gradual Release of Responsibility Model because it allows students to be apprentices, to be kids who are learning the writing process step-by-step, sentence-by-sentence, stage-by-stage, one paragraph at a time.

First LeBron learned how to dribble. Then LeBron learned how to shoot. Then LeBron learned how to box out, rebound, and move his feet on defense.

Then LeBron creatively discovered an individual, dynamic way to put it all together, empowering him to become a veritable Picasso on an NBA floor.

Deliberate Practice: What It is, Why It's Effective

It goes without saying that getting enough practice writing is absolutely required for developing strong writers. And not just practice, mind you, but deliberate practice. What's the difference?

Practice is grabbing a basketball and shooting jump shots for 45 minutes.

Deliberate practice is pivoting in the low post and shooting a five-foot bank shot off the glass 50 times in a row, having a coach help you make appropriate adjustments along the way to your footwork, shooting stroke, and body position in order to improve the percentage of baskets you make.

Practice is nebulous; deliberate practice is precise. According to psychologist and scientific researcher, Dr. K. Anders Ericsson, one of the foremost scholars on deliberate practice, studies show time and again that the quality of practice is just as important as the quantity of practice.

Embedding Ericsson's ideas into the instruction of writing can move mountains.

Too much of modern writing instruction falls victim to just being practice as opposed to being deliberate, quality practice that purposely focuses on improving precisely defined, chunked, standards-based skills.

My own personal feeling is that too much of modern writing instruction falls victim to just being practice as opposed to being deliberate, quality practice that purposely focuses on improving precisely defined, chunked, standards-based skills. Right now, we very often assign one long writing task that asks students to demonstrate mastery over eight different standards-based skills at the same time (general practice) as opposed to assigning eight different writing assignments that ask students to demonstrate mastery over one unique standards-based skill one step at a time (deliberate practice).

Making this shift allows writing teachers to work smarter, not harder, and better sets the stage for driving measurable growth once kids learn the tools to put it all together.

Of course, the phrase "quality practice" can be a slippery term to define as it varies from student to student based on things like a child's prior knowledge, their current acumen, and so on. So what is "quality practice"?

The Comfort Zone, the Learning Zone, and the Panic Zone

Noel Tichy, former chief of General Electric's famous management development center at Crotonville and professor at the University of Michigan School of Business, divides the concept of practice into three different zones: the Comfort Zone, the Learning Zone, and the Panic Zone.

The Learning Zone is where students encounter quality practice. (Yes, for those of you who were paying attention in graduate school, Tichy is standing on the shoulders of Vygotsky's Zone of Proximal Development. A rose by any other name, right?)

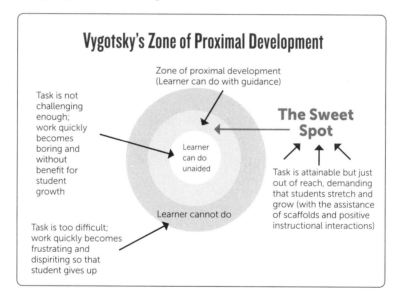

Tichy realized that, when it came to practice, most people stayed within their comfort zone, particularly if they were not being led by a strong teacher or coach. (Hello, student reflection journals, can you hear me?) Comfort Zone practice, Tichy notes, doesn't really help people improve because students can already do the activities easily. Also, poor habits tend to be reinforced. (This is why Lil' Timmy keeps neglecting to indent paragraphs over and over and over again—because he's "practiced" doing it the wrong way far too many times.)

On the other hand, thrusting a student into the Panic Zone can leave a person paralyzed because the demands are too challenging. When feelings of inadequacy become too great, confidence plummets, frustration mounts, and students get dispirited to the point that giving up feels like a better option than continuing to try.

Throw kids with low skills into the deep end of a dark pool knowing that their ability to swim is suspect and the only thing that's really being developed is a sense of intense fear that they might drown. And when they gurgle their way back to the side of the pool, coughing up water, feeling threatened and even ashamed at their lack of actual abilities in the water, very few of them are eager and excited to jump back into the water and try again.

Great writing performance is a by-product of great writing practice.

Tichy says the only way for students to make progress is to operate in the Learning Zone, a space where activities are graspable but just out of reach and require stretching to attain—but are attainable. Great writing performance is a by-product of great writing practice. Deliberate practice, to be exact, that takes place inside the Learning Zone.

Exposure to Models: What It is, Why It's Effective

While many an ELA teacher has dueled for resources, classroom minutes, the principal's attention, and so on, with math people, we have to give credit where it's due: math folks are the original modelers.

Think about the way you learned addition, subtraction, multiplication, division, algebra, geometry, or beyond. For me, it came through seeing a teacher write an equation on the board and then watching the instructor do a think-aloud that demonstrated the process of solving the problem step-by-step.

They showed me an example. They talked me through each of the parts. They increased my abilities by starting with foundational skills and then they put me on a mathematical escalator that ascended, the degree of task complexity growing more difficult as I gained mastery over the material that I'd preciously been taught.

And then, like it or not, they made me practice and practice until I had it down cold.

Newsflash: learning requires hard work! To convey any other message does a disservice to kids. Now, of course, hard work and strong effort are not mutually exclusive from joy; they can easily go hand in hand (and should, whenever possible).

Yet, as far as modeling is concerned, Donald Murray said, "Writing might be magical, but it's not magic. It's a process, a rational series of decisions and steps that every writer makes and takes."

Studying models allows young writers to transparently see the "rational series of decisions and steps that every writer makes and takes." In fact, studying models of strong short-response writing has many benefits.

By using models to improve skills, students can:

▶ see and discuss the qualities that make good writing effective.

▶ identify elements that work especially well for different types of writing tasks . . . and do not work as well with different types of tasks.

▶ feel as if they are a part of a classroom community of writers (and not merely isolated, individual toilers struggling with the art of composing).

▶ hear and see the teacher model fluency and expression in reading text as well as writing text through attention to things like intonation, inflection, and vocabulary, as well as grammar, punctuation, and word choice.

▶ overtly illuminate aspects of "the writer's toolkit," which are widely available for all students to use and have been proven to succeed.

Enabling kids to participate in think-alouds that are aligned to standards-based instructional aims has many benefits. The biggest benefit may be that using models is an excellent means for building students' background knowledge.

This is *huge*! Truly, its importance can't be overemphasized. In *The Comprehension Toolkit*, by Stephanie Harvey and Anne Goudvis, the authors say that everything we learn is colored by our background knowledge. As Dr. Bob Marzano says in his book *Building Background Knowledge for Academic Achievement* (yes, he wrote a whole book on it), "What students already know about the content is one of the strongest indicators of how well they will learn new information relative to the content." Heck, Fountas and Pinnell's entire body of awesomeness with their leveled-reading programs is predicated on taking into consideration the student's background knowledge prior to matching the child with a text.

Models are a proven and well-supported asset. Use them. As writing instructors, there are two particular types especially worth incorporating in order to improve outcomes: Read-Alouds and Write-Alouds.

READ-ALOUD (or modeled reading): when a teacher does a planned oral reading of a text in front of students usually related to a theme or a topic of study.

WRITE-ALOUD (or modeled writing): when a teacher executes a planned writing task in front of students transparently illuminating the techniques, frameworks, and behaviors he or she utilizes in order to achieve success.

As ReadWriteThink.org states, "Research has demonstrated that students improve their writing ability when cognitive strategies are demonstrated for them in clear and explicit ways. Students learn the forms and functions of writing as they observe and participate in writing events directed by knowledgeable writers, particularly when these events are followed by opportunities for independent writing. Instruction that makes writing processes visible to students is key to improving their writing skills."

CHAPTER 3

Introducing Triple C Writing:

Claim It! Cite It! Cement It!

This is a great time to shatter the false notion of "the natural-born writer." Please, for your sake and the sake of the children, do away with this wrong-headed idea immediately because to accept that there are natural-born writers is to imply that there are also natural-born nonwriters.

No one is born a writer. Writing is a learned skill.

Now, do some kids have an affinity, some talent? Sure. But, for the most part, without proper cultivation, nothing much will ever come of it. (And please spare us the prodigy example of a kid on a mountaintop with a half-chewed pencil made from goat marrow who evolves into Rumi; I am talking about teaching millions of perfectly well-penciled students in Baltimore, Miami, Milwaukee, Dallas, Los Angeles, and so on.)

Of course, we do have to concede that some kids come to school with challenges that hamper their ability to develop their writing skills—or perform well in any subject at all. These factors, to name a few, include:

- ▶ socioeconomic disadvantages

- ▶ language challenges

- ▶ special needs

- ▶ detrimental home environments

- ▶ a past characterized by educators who have shamed them and helped to create stigmas around their low writing skills

Personally, I've worked with kids who've entered my class with horrible histories of abuse, neglect, violence, and so on, and I'd be lying if I said that I bat 1.000 with these students by any stretch of the imagination. As I've said before, mitigating factors outside the classroom affect student performance inside the classroom, and anyone who tells you differently has either never been on the front lines of American education or is trying to sell you something.

So, do I believe that *all* students in your class right now CAN learn how to write well? Yes! Will it be easy? No, there is no magic wand.

Big picture: Using the Three Cs—the details of which are on their way in the next chapter—is a proven system of constructing short responses that delivers excellent results.

One important tidbit to be aware of right now, however, is that the bulk of the process rests on architectural design. In other words, it's about understanding that success with the writer's craft is built on structure, a structure that is learned through a combination of explicit instruction, exposure to models, and deliberate practice.

Structure, Principles of Design, and Success Systems

Mention the word *structure* as it applies to teaching students how to write well and some people go cuckoo. I don't know why. The fact is, a huge proportion of the most beloved writing of all time is anchored in structure.

Fiction has structure. Plots not only have beginnings, middles, and ends, but, as Joseph Campbell illuminated in *The Hero With a Thousand Faces*, structure underpins almost every culture on the planet's most impactful, enduring tales.

"A hero ventures forth from the world of common day into a region of supernatural wonder: fabulous forces are there encountered and a decisive victory is won: The hero comes back from this mysterious adventure with the power to bestow boons on his fellow man." (Campbell, 1949)

Walt Disney's tales were anchored in structure. As are the works of Alexandre Dumas, Jules Verne, Fyodor Dostoyevsky, John Grisham, Harper Lee, and John Green (even if it had not yet been named at the time of their writing). Take a gander at so many of our most classic, canonical stories and you'll see that, yes, there's a recognizable "Hero's Journey" structure common to them all. Why? Because when fiction writers use structure to underpin their work, it's a smart decision.

But does this means that only fiction writing ought to tap the power of structure to enhance its chances of success?

Journalists use structure. From pyramid writing to not burying the lede, and so on, there are formulas for producing rock-solid nonfiction writing that characterize good practice. As there are for corporate copywriters, grant writers, business plan writers, technical writers, computer code writers, and résumé writers.

We could go through category after category to illustrate how structure underpins strong writing practice, but let's not lose sight of the forest for the trees; for the most part when it comes to teaching writing to kids, any mention of the word *structure* automatically gets conflated with the idea of stifled creativity and formulaic blandness.

Providing students with the intellectual equipment necessary to bring the critical elements of strong architecture to their writing doesn't clip their wings; it gives them a rock-solid structural design that empowers them to successfully communicate their thinking. And writers, especially developing writers, benefit tremendously from having this toolkit/recipe/methodology/system/procedure—call it whatever you want. A *Washington Post* op-ed piece said it oh-so-well:

Expository writing skills simply haven't been taught in many elementary schools for the past 30 years or so. Instead, what has been taught, at some schools, is self-expression: stories, poems, personal essays. That approach may get kids to embrace the idea of writing, but it doesn't teach them how to write. One of my students showed me a poem she composed that was so powerful it took my breath away, but she couldn't write a logical paragraph to save her life.

(from https://www.washingtonpost.com/opinions/if-students-cant-write-how-can-they-learn/2013/11/01/48165da0-36ab-11e3-80c6-7e6dd8d22d8f_story.html)

. . . . . .

Since the proven principles for how to successfully compose an argumentative or expository short response have already been unlocked, why not teach these tools to your students to help them develop their thinking skills?

This is a *huge* point. Ultimately, writing is a tool for the expression of thought and the sooner students know *how* to write well, the sooner teachers can focus in on *what* they have written.

Said another way, after building capable composers who own strong, foundational writing skills, the lion's share of an educator's instructional time can be spent building deeper thinkers.

Now that's a big win!

Ultimately, writing is a tool for the expression of thought and the sooner students know how to write well, the sooner teachers can focus in on what they have written.

Using the Three Cs: Claim It! Cite It! Cement It!

To become strong writers—and thinkers—kids need to be writing. A lot. Why? Because writing allows people to more clearly see what it is they actually think. For example, here's a pop quiz:

> A visitor just came to your home city and wants your suggestion about the top five restaurants they should eat at while they're in town for the next two weeks. What's your answer?

If you try and respond to this solely in your head without the benefit of pen and paper, number one and number two probably pop into your brain fairly easily. But then, as you mentally move down the list, choices three, four, and five get a little fuzzy.

However, if you grab a pencil and write down your top restaurant suggestions, BOOM, after a moment, you produce a solid answer.

"These are my top five!" you say with confidence.

Why? Because writing forces people to crystallize their thinking and make firm decisions. Having to "ink" clear choices forces a person to focus their mind and produces concrete outcomes. This is why writing is so beneficial. It transforms abstract notions into tangible concepts.

Professor Timothy Shanahan, one of the nation's leading thinkers on literacy, put it this way: "I suspect the reason for this is that writing forces one to think through an idea more thoroughly. There are many times when I start to write a blog entry, thinking I know what I want to say, but as I compose, the limitations of my thinking are exposed—in a way that speaking does not seem to do."

Writing is thought made manifest.

WHAT THE RESEARCH SAYS

Is the assertion that "one of the smartest ways to spend your precious classroom minutes is to concentrate on building rock-solid short-response writers" a research-based claim? After all, what does the data say about time, effort, and energy spent honing student writing skills? Is the idea that "learning to write good is good for students" based on concrete evidence or is this idea just being pulled out of a hat?

Good news, the research is pretty much unequivocal: as a pedagogical practice, writing rocks!

Vanderbilt University's Professor Stephen Graham and Michael Hiebert wrote a report for the Carnegie Foundation that scrutinized data from more than 100 studies. Here are four significant findings they took from their meta-analysis:

1. Writing about text has a strong, positive effect on reading comprehension.

2. Writing about text is clearly better than just reading the text.

3. Writing about text is clearly better than reading and then rereading the text.

4. Writing about text is clearly better than reading and then talking about the text.

This is the kind of juicy research that gets education folks all tingly on the inside because a straight line is being drawn from A to B.

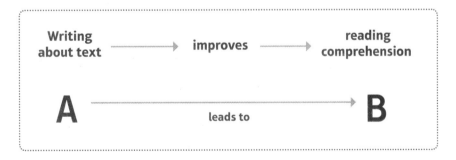

FOLLOWING THE LEAD OF EXPERT INSTRUCTORS

Lucy Calkins is a lion in the world of writing instruction. She is the Founding Director of the Teachers College Reading and Writing Project, a bestselling author, and an innovative educator who popularized the Writer's Workshop across America. If there were a Hall of Fame for Teachers of Writing, Lucy Calkins would be a first ballot shoe-in. Literally, casting a vote for her would be akin to voting for Babe Ruth, Joe DiMaggio, or Willie Mays. Many are good; Lucy Calkins is *great*.

The following quote by Calkins has particularly informed the development of Triple C Writing:

> "The image of a routine for writing is not just about sitting down to write. A writing routine involves understanding what it means to work at your writing."
>
> **—LUCY CALKINS**

Why is this quote so significant? First, it validates the idea that writers build their skills by having a routine, one that is well-considered and works intelligently toward reaching a specific, measurable goal.

Success in building rock-solid short-response writers through Triple C Writing rests on implementing a proven, research-based approach to achievement. Indeed, it's user-friendly and adaptable to each individual student's needs, but there is a science underpinning Triple C Writing, and one of its critical anchors is creating a routine.

As previously mentioned, we don't just practice, we deliberately practice with a precise, measurable goal explicitly at the forefront of our aims. That's the first part of what Calkins means by "working at your writing."

Calkins' "working at your writing" quote also speaks to a second idea: namely, the most effective way for students to do this is to chunk the process. Who knows better than Lucy Calkins that teaching a student to write well takes time? And who knows better that scaffolded lessons that build upon prior successes, one upon another, are the smartest, surest path to developing lifelong abilities?

Stripped to its most essential level, strong writers know that words have specific jobs, sentences have specific jobs, and paragraphs have specific jobs. Thus, Triple C Writing makes sure that students fully and completely understand each of the aforementioned roles. Once your young writers do, they will be well on their way to moving from the apprentice stage toward becoming master craftspersons.

Yes, that's a big claim. But also, it's entirely achievable.

MOVING ON TO THE FIRST C: CLAIM IT!

One final thought to keep in mind: all kids are different. Some will take to Triple C Writing like a duck to water and other kids might take to it like a duck to pâté. What's worth noting is that no part of this should be presented to students as any sort of race against an artificially constructed clock of achievement. In fact, what's most important is that students come to the process of becoming rock-solid writers bearing in mind the following words.

> *Stripped to its most essential level, strong writers know that words have specific jobs, sentences have specific jobs, and paragraphs have specific jobs. Thus, Triple C Writing makes sure that students fully and completely understand each of the afore-mentioned roles.*

"It does not matter how slowly you go as long as you do not stop."

—CONFUCIUS

CHAPTER 4

The First C:
Claim It!

We live in a land of claims. From teachers ("homework is important"), to students ("homework is lame"), to parents ("brussels sprouts are good for you"), to politicians ("we need to lower taxes on brussels sprouts"), and on and on. Few, if any of us, can make it through a 24-hour cycle without being exposed to a voluminous amount of claims.

Claims bombard us from all angles. Some are informative ("building capable young writers is imperative"), some are spiritual ("there are no accidents in the universe; you are exactly where you are supposed to be right at this very moment"), and some are downright fraudulent ("your long-lost uncle just passed and if you'd kindly send me your social security number, date of birth, and bank account number, 16.2 million dollars will promptly be deposited into your checking account").

In fact, teaching students to make claims is pretty easy because they are already doing it every day.

"I deserve a new cell phone."

"It's not fair that I have to clean up my sister's mess."

"Just because I am covered in dirt does not mean I need a bath!"

The Six Action Steps for Making a Claim

Here are the six Action Steps you can use to teach young writers how to clearly, concisely, and cogently "claim it!"

The Instructional Action Steps

ACTION STEP **1** ▶ **DETERMINE** Where Your Students Are (Baseline Measurement)

ACTION STEP **2** ▶ **DEFINE** What a Claim Is (And What It Is Not!)

ACTION STEP **3** ▶ **DEMONSTRATE** How to Make a Claim (Front of Class Write-Aloud)

ACTION STEP **4** ▶ **TASK** Students With Making a Claim

ACTION STEP **5** ▶ **DEMONSTRATE** How to Revise a Claim (Front of Class Write-Aloud)

ACTION STEP **6** ▶ **TASK** Students With Revising Their Claim

ACTION STEP 1: Determine Where Your Students Are (Baseline Measurement)

As mindfulness author Jon Kabat-Zinn is fond of saying, "Wherever you go, there you are." This is why we begin with a baseline measurement: we need to know exactly where kids are, right here and right now. All of us hold ideas about where students should be, but until we see some hard, tangible work on the page, none of us can say with certainty where our students actually are in terms of their abilities to write a cogent, coherent short response.

Therefore, just like an aspiring dieter on New Year's Day must actually step onto a scale to document a concrete starting weight before commencing on their new Beverly Hills Garbanzo Bean and Honey Covered Red Ant Gluten Free Papaya Diet, so, too, must our students record a literal measurement of their present abilities.

Warning: Don't coach. Don't preteach or provide any instruction at all. Just give your kids a straightforward, "Okay, it's time to see where we are" moment of truth on the writing scales. By definition, taking a baseline assessment of student performance means that we'll need to gather an accurate measurement of their aptitudes *before* any teaching occurs. This allows everyone to attain a true data set on the effect of the teaching. If educators instruct before they measure, the process goes kablooey.

Ultimately, the baseline measure provides for you a means to be able to prove that, "On this date, the student's abilities were here and now, on this date, you can see that the student's abilities are, as a result of working with the process outlined in this book, here . . . and what a difference!"

Of course, administrators love seeing concrete evidence of measurable growth. Teachers, too, love seeing concrete evidence of measurable growth. But never forget, the people who most love seeing concrete evidence of measurable growth are the students themselves. Students who never believed they'd earn accolades for their writing skills will be absolutely thrilled to see proof of their newly developed acumen.

Here are a few sample prompts that are easily accessible to all students. (Remember, do not offer any directives about quality, length, textual evidence, grammar, and so on.)

▶ What is the most interesting animal in nature?

▶ What popular athlete or movie star would probably make a good President of the United States?

▶ When it comes to telling a story, what's better, movies, books, or television shows?

▶ Since Dr. Seuss wasn't a real doctor, should he have been allowed to call himself Dr. Seuss?

A Quick Tip of the Cap to Toulmin

Professor Stephen Toulmin, a 20th century philosopher, became frustrated with the inability of formal logic to explain everyday arguments. He called it the Toulmin Model of Argumentation and without a doubt, *Mastering Short-Response Writing: Claim It! Cite It! Cement It!* is standing squarely on the shoulders of Toulmin's work. (High fives are in order.)

ACTION STEP 2: Define What a Claim Is (And What It Is Not!)

The word *claim* comes from the Latin word *clamare*, which means "to cry out, shout."

- ▶ Kids prefer ice cream over cupcakes.
- ▶ Playing tic-tac-toe is fun.
- ▶ Math is an important skill to have in life.

These are claims. For young writers, defining what a claim is in a manner that is simple, straightforward, and free of jargon is our starting point.

Student-friendly definition of what it means to Claim It:
A claim is when someone says, "this is true"—it's when a person puts forth an idea that something is an actual fact.

Now hold the phone, because a claim is NOT a statement of fact; a claim is when someone asserts that something is a fact—and there is a HUGE difference between the two.

This is why when teaching your students what a claim is, you also want to teach them what a claim is not. Remember, a claim is an assertion of truth but it is not the truth. Claims must be debatable. For example:

This is a claim	This is *not* a claim
McDonald's French fries are delicious.	McDonald's French fries are a type of food.
The author of the story likes furry animals.	The author wrote a story about furry animals.
Go Fish! is a fun and simple card game.	Go Fish! is a card game.

Make sure students understand the debatable nature of claims. When a person says, "Football is a more entertaining sport than baseball," that is a claim. When a person says, "Football is a sport," that is not a claim. Why? Because the latter is a nondebatable statement of fact.

Here are a few more examples you can use with your students:

This is a claim	This is *not* a claim
Nikes are more fashionable than Reeboks.	Nike makes shoes for running.
The bus driver cares about his passengers.	The bus driver is paid to transport passengers.
Television was a horrible invention.	Television broadcasts many different shows.

After being given a few well-chosen examples, most students will see how not every statement is a claim, an important distinction that will serve them as the demands of their assignments grow more complex.

The Four Types of Claims

Claims typically fall into one of four categories.

Claims of fact or definition

These claims argue about what the definition of something is or whether something is a settled fact.

EXAMPLE: *Playing too many video games is bad for children's health.*

Claims of cause and effect

These claims argue that one person, thing, or event caused another thing or event to occur.

EXAMPLE: *The popularity of video games has caused childhood obesity to increase.*

Claims about value

These are claims made about what something is worth, whether we value it or not.

EXAMPLE: *The widespread popularity of video games is one of the most troubling issues facing parents today.*

Claims about solutions or policies

These are claims that argue for or against a certain solution or policy approach to a problem.

EXAMPLE: *Instead of allowing kids to play video games, we should focus on ways to get them off of their screens and out into nature.*

Going Deeper: Expository Versus Argumentative Claims

There are two different types of claims on which this material focuses: expository and argumentative. While the overall structure for both is similar, each type of short response has its own specific aim.

Expository Short Response	Argumentative Short Response
Aims to explain, describe, or inform an audience	Aims to convince or sway an audience
Focuses on facts	Focuses on judgments
Unbiased and objective	Biased and subjective
Tells how or why	Tells what to think or believe

Remind your students that expository claims aim to explain or describe. They are often neutral and unbiased and tell an audience how or why. On the other hand, argumentative claims aim to convince or sway (through evidence; more on that in the next chapter). They are biased and subjective, telling others what to think or believe.

ACTION STEP 3: Demonstrate How to Make a Claim (Front-of-Class Write-Aloud)

"Write-Alouds" (also known as modeled writing) allow the teacher to share her thinking as she composes a piece of writing in front of her kids. It enables inexperienced student writers to bear witness to the "moves" a strong writer makes while writing. This "transparent modeling" improves students' understanding of the writing process and ultimately translates into elevated learner performance.

In fact, the Write-Aloud offers many benefits. To name a few:

▶ It makes the writing process observable and concrete.

▶ It enables students to see how no one, not even their teacher, is "perfect."

▶ It allows a teacher to more easily check to see if her students are successfully adopting the specific techniques and strategies she featured in her Write-Aloud lesson once students' begin to compose their own independent work.

▶ It sends a strong message that everyone, even the teacher, must revise in order to improve his or her work.

DRAFTING YOUR WRITE-ALOUD CLAIM IN FRONT OF STUDENTS

When writing aloud, be sure to start with fairly simple claims to ensure that students understand what a claim is.

Here are some Write-Alouds you might want to try:

Make a claim about something in the classroom.

▶ If we paint these walls green, it will help students feel more comfortable.

▶ The door of this classroom needs to be wider.

▶ Instead of putting up student work on the walls, we should put up pictures of underwater life.

Make a claim about something to do with food.

▶ Pretzels are the best snack ever invented.

- ▸ Students eat too much pizza.
- ▸ Not enough chocolate-covered ants are eaten by American kids.

Make a claim about something to do with animals.

- ▸ Dolphins are cuter than kittens.
- ▸ Squirrels are better climbers than spiders.
- ▸ Birds make for terrible pets.

Now that you have illuminated the difference between a claim and a statement of fact and done a few Write-Alouds for the sake of modeling, it's time to hand the steering wheel over to the students.

ACTION STEP 4: Task Students With Making a Claim

It's teacher choice on this one. You can have students call and respond, you can have students independently write down claims and then call and respond, you can break your class into collaborative learning groups and have each team of students create one claim about anything from the quality of the food being served on campus to the importance of exercise. As mentioned previously, you know your students better than anyone else, so follow your inner star on this one.

ACTION STEP **5**: Demonstrate How to Revise a Claim

It's time to revise your claim in front of all your students to show them the power of revision. The earlier you start to pound the drum that writers constantly rewrite the better. Part of the way that this gets achieved is by showing them that all writers revise. Even the President of the United States!

The following is one of my favorite "revision" pictures of all time. The writer: Barack Obama. The composition: a State of the Union speech mere hours before he is set to deliver it to Congress and the nation.

Sharing images like this lets the entire class know, "Everyone revises. It's the only way to be successful."

By revising for the whole class, you show students how writers use the process of revision to make their claims more crisp (the idea being that sharper, crisper claims result in better, stronger contentions).

> **Some Ideas for Revision** *(Taken From the Examples Above)*
>
> Dolphins are cuter than kittens.
>
> > *Can change to . . .*
>
> Bottlenose dolphins are cuter than hairless kittens.
>
> (Opportunity to teach adjectives.)
>
> Squirrels are better climbers of trees than spiders.
>
> > *Can change to . . .*
>
> Squirrels climb trees better than spiders.
>
> (Opportunity to teach active verbs.)
>
> Birds make for bad pets.
>
> > *Can change to . . .*
>
> Parakeets make for bad pets.
>
> (Opportunity to teach the value of specificity.)

Editing vs. Revision

Many people often use the terms "editing" and "revision" interchangeably, but the two are very distinct. Editing focuses on getting the grammar, spelling, and punctuation right, while revision focuses on reworking the ideas being presented, their strengths, weaknesses, organization, and so on.

Because many students may struggle with editing their claims, you might want to consider a few purposeful misspellings or punctuation mistakes for some good teaching opportunities and to show that no one is immune.

Maybe your Write-Alouds look a bit like this (by design):

▶ Dolphins are cutter than kittens.

▶ Squirrels are beter climbers than spiders.

▶ Birds make 4 terrible pets.

ACTION STEP **6**: Task Students With Revising Their Claims

You may want to have some students come to the front of the room and share a "before and after" for everyone to see, or maybe you can visit each of your collaborative groupings to see how kids went from A to B in their teams. The options for instruction are plentiful—the only real "rule" is that *all* claims must be revised. And every claim can be revised—make sure students dive back in.

Birds make for bad pets.

Can change to . . .

Parakeets make for bad pets.

Can change to . . .

Parakeets make bad pets.

Can change to . . .

Parakeets make dreadful pets.

Can change to . . .

Baby parakeets make dreadful pets.

Can change to . . .

Baby parakeets from the northern coast of Brazil make dreadful pets.

And the beat goes on . . .

Hone the Three Core Skills
of Successful Claim-Making

It's now time for students to start individually tackling claims—first by reading and evaluating them. For students to become strong claim makers, they need to be sturdy evaluators of what strong claim-making looks like. (As well as what poor claim-making looks like . . . we'll do both.)

This is where all the positive research regarding the deep, beneficial connection between reading and writing turns from theory to practice. By asking students to first read a claim, either yours or one of the claims that they've written, and then evaluate it through a set of three different lenses, they gain a much better understanding of the core ingredients necessary to author their own well-written claims.

The Three Claim It! Lenses

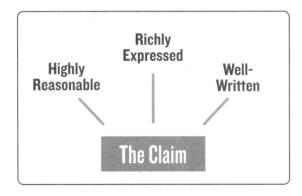

WHAT IS A HIGHLY REASONABLE CLAIM?

Before asking students to make highly reasonable claims, overtly define for them what the task "make a highly reasonable claim" means.

A highly reasonable claim is one that stays within the realm of common sense; it's rational, logical, and of sound thought process.

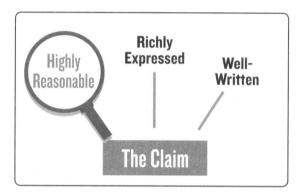

Example:

Highly Reasonable Claim	Unreasonable Claim
The school should offer students time each day to relax, play, and reenergize.	The school should cancel all learning so that students can spend all day relaxing, playing, and reenergizing.
Teachers ought to expect that parents will sometimes help their kids with homework.	Teachers ought to expect that parents will do all their kids' homework for them.

Ask students to make a reasonable claim about . . .

  ▶ the best type of vacation for a family to take.

  ▶ the worst type of restaurant to eat at if you are a kid.

  ▶ the importance of cleaning your room.

For each claim, ask students to give themselves a score, from 1–3:

- ▶ 3 points if their claim makes good sense
- ▶ 2 points if their claim sort of makes sense
- ▶ 1 point if their claim makes little to no sense

GATEKEEPING CHECKPOINT: Though only three examples have been provided, you might want to assign as many as 20 different claims. Continue to assign the "Make a highly reasonable claim about" task until you feel your students are rock-solid and ready to move on.

WHAT IS A RICHLY EXPRESSED CLAIM?

Before asking students to write a richly expressed claim, it's best to define for them what the task "write a richly expressed claim" means.

A richly expressed claim is one that has some *POP!* It's a claim with energy, zip, and zest.

Example:

Richly Expressed Claim	Dull Claim
It's critical that teachers send the clear message that bullying will not be tolerated at school.	Bullying is bad and teachers should tell that to the kids.
Serving vanilla-and-chocolate-swirl-flavored ice cream cake adds an extra dash of awesomeness to a kid's birthday party.	Ice cream cake is good to serve at birthday parties.

Ask students to make a richly expressed claim about . . .

▶ the best breakfast to serve a six-year-old.

▶ the most fun game to play with a group of three other friends.

▶ the worst thing about a rainy day.

For each claim, ask students to give themselves a score, from 1–3:

▶ 3 points if this claim packs a nice POP!

▶ 2 points if this claim gets the job done

▶ 1 point if this claim has little to no energy

GATEKEEPING CHECKPOINT: Though only three examples have been provided, you might want to assign as many as 20 different claims. Continue to assign the "Make a richly expressed claim about" task until you feel your students are rock-solid and ready to move on.

WHAT IS A WELL-WRITTEN CLAIM?

Before asking students to write a well-written claim, it's best to overtly define for them what the task "write a well-written claim" means.

A well-written claim pays close attention to the details of execution and demonstrates careful writing; it makes sure that things such as spelling, grammar, and punctuation have been carefully considered—and proofread—by the writer.

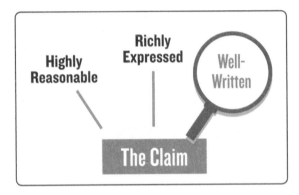

Example:

Carelessly Written Claim	Well-Written Claim
Doctors say that eating to much candy is detrimental for a childs helth.	Doctors agree that eating too much candy is detrimental to a child's health.
Sleepover partys can b fun but usually a kid doesnt, get 2 much sleep	Sleepover parties can be fun, but usually a kid doesn't get too much sleep.

Basic Editing Checklist

It's time to check the important elements such as spelling, grammar, punctuation, capitalization, and subject-verb agreement. While this probably will not be a student writer's favorite step in the writing process, it's an important one!

Capitalization

- ▶ Each sentence starts with a capital letter.
- ▶ All names of people and places begin with a capital letter.
- ▶ Titles in a person's name begin with a capital letter.
- ▶ Each important word in a title begins with a capital letter.

Punctuation

- ▶ Quotation marks surround all words that are part of a direct quote.
- ▶ Commas separate items in a list.
- ▶ All sentences end with a period or other appropriate ending punctuation.

Spelling and Sentences

- ▶ Words are spelled correctly. If you are using a computer, remember to use the spell-check function.
- ▶ All sentences are complete and include a subject and a verb.
- ▶ All subjects and verbs agree.

Ask students to make a well-written claim about . . .

- ▶ the worst thing to give a kid for a birthday present.
- ▶ the scariest character ever to appear in a movie.
- ▶ what pets can teach people about relationships.

For each claim, ask students to give themselves a score, from 1–3:

- ▶ 3 points if this claim is error-free
- ▶ 2 points if this claim has a mistake or two
- ▶ 1 point if this claim has multiple mistakes

GATEKEEPING CHECKPOINT: Though only three examples have been provided, you might want to assign as many as 20 different claims. Continue to assign the "Make a well-written claim about" task until you feel your students are rock-solid and ready to move on.

Synthesize the Instruction: Students Craft Highly Reasonable, Richly Expressed, Well-Written Claims

Now that students have refined their skills in each of the three domains, it's time to have them put it all together. This is the moment at which a teacher can start to expect a higher level of acumen and achievement.

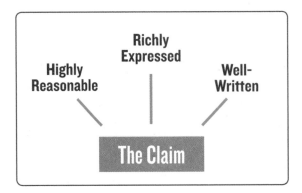

Whenever your students compose a claim from this point forward, you can rightly expect high levels of achievement. Be overt, be direct, be encouraging, but also be uncompromising: all claims from this point forward must be reasonable, richly expressed, and well written. No excuses. And if students need to revise their claims over and over again to get them right, so be it!

Tips for Elevating Performance

Here are a few tips to share with your students—as well as a few pitfalls to consciously avoid—that will empower your kids to write strong, rock-solid claims.

ANSWER THE QUESTION BEING ASKED

If I had a nickel for every time a student answered the question they assumed was being asked as opposed to the one that was actually being asked, I'd have a lot of coins. As would most teachers.

Be overt about the fact that one of the major pitfalls many students stumble over when it comes to writing rock-solid claims is that they respond to a question that is different from the one posed to them.

For example:

QUESTION: What is the best type of fish to buy for a five-year-old who's never owned a pet before?

ANSWER: Getting a five-year-old a new puppy, a yellow Labrador retriever, is definitely the best choice for a pet.

Um, hello? The question asked what was the best type of fish.

Answer the question being asked!

BETTER ANSWER: When it comes to the best type of fish to buy a five-year-old as a first pet, it's really hard to beat a goldfish.

TAKE A CLEAR POSITION (NO WAFFLING!)

If I had another nickel for every time a young writer hedged, hemmed, hawed, and tried to say "this but that" inside their claim, I'd have a lot more coins. As would most teachers.

For advanced debaters discussing sophisticated notions that are filled with mitigating complexities, by all means it's entirely appropriate to meld nuance into claim-making. However, just like Picasso learned how to draw still lifes before he painted the iconic masterpiece *Guernica*, so too must novice writers master the art of taking an apparent, unequivocal position.

In other words, make sure your students take a clear side, stake their claim, and firmly assert one unambiguous stance.

For example:

QUESTION: What is the best type of after-school snack to serve to an eight-year-old?

ANSWER: Serving pretzels always is one good choice for an after-school snack, but a nice piece of fruit or even a cold popsicle is a good idea as well.

Um, hello? The question asked you for the best snack.

Make a clear, unambiguous choice! (It strengthens the claim.)

BETTER ANSWER: When it comes to the best after-school snack to serve to an eight-year-old, there's nothing better than a healthy piece of delicious fruit.

REPEAT THE KEY WORDS OF THE QUESTION IN THE ANSWER

There is no more direct and concise way of answering a question than using the "meat" of the question as the core phrase in an answer. This is not cheating. This is not copying. (Well, it is, but it's legal and advisable.) This is just what rock-solid writers who compose strong claims do. Have your students do it as well.

For example:

QUESTION: What is the most delicious but least healthy snack you sometimes eat at lunch?

ANSWER: I eat sour cream and onion potato chips at lunch.

Um, hello? The opportunity to write a much stronger claim is staring you right in the face.

BETTER ANSWER: The most delicious but least healthy snack I sometimes eat at lunch is sour cream and onion potato chips.

Use the key phrases and vocabulary of the question as part of your response in order to improve your work!

Moving On to the Second C: Cite It!

As a teacher, you have now arrived at a fork in the road. Do you feel as if your students own the crisp, clean, strong claim-making skills they need to have in order to matriculate to the next stage of Triple C Writing? Or do you feel that they still need more deliberate practice on a specific element such as punctuation, voice, vocabulary, and so on?

Warning: Don't make this a race against an artificial clock. If your students need another week to better lock in their use of smartly chosen adverbs, then by all means, take the time now to do a few more whole-class lessons on adverbs. Moving on when you know most kids in your room are not able to compose a well-written claim—which is only one sentence, mind you—sets you up for problems down the line when we expand the volume of their output while insisting on the same degree of quality.

In other words, the expectations that their written ideas are reasonable, richly expressed, and well-written never get taken off the table. Now that we have put them on, they stay there . . . for the rest of their life!

Moving on? *Congrats!* Well done.

Need to circle back for a little more refinement? *Congrats* as well! It takes a brave teacher to serve the students as opposed to the "agenda."

CHAPTER 5

The Second C:
Cite It!

With so many people making so many claims about so many things, how in the world do we know which claims are worth believing? This is where evidence comes in.

People don't just want to know what you believe; people want to know how you know what you believe in order to determine whether or not they should accept your claim.

In other words, don't just claim it, cite it!

If your claim is something you think is true, your evidence is the proof that your thinking makes sense. It's the support that demonstrates whether or not the claim holds merit.

The Instructional Action Steps

ACTION STEP **1** ▶ **DETERMINE** Where Your Students Are (Baseline Measurement)

ACTION STEP **2** ▶ **DEFINE** What It Means to Cite It! (And Why It Is So Important)

ACTION STEP **3** ▶ **DEMONSTRATE** How to Cite It! (Front-of-Class Write-Aloud)

ACTION STEP **4** ▶ **TASK** Students With Citing Evidence to Support Their Claim

ACTION STEP **5** ▶ **DEMONSTRATE** How to Revise a Citation of Evidence

ACTION STEP **6** ▶ **TASK** Students With Revising Their Citation of Evidence

ACTION STEP **1**: Determine Where Your Students Are (Baseline Measurement)

The Second C (Cite It!) follows the same series of Instructional Action Steps as the first C (Claim It!) beginning with a baseline measurement so that we can determine exactly where our students are in terms of their ability to cite relevant, strong, accurate evidence to support their claims.

Remember: At this point, we do not want to coach or preteach or provide any instruction regarding how to cite evidence. For now, simply give your kids a straightforward, "okay, it's time to see where we are" moment of truth after assigning them a task that asks them to support their claim with reasoning.

Here are a few sample prompts you may want to use. (Remember, do not offer any directives about quality, length, textual evidence, grammar, and so on.)

▶ What is the most dangerous animal in nature and why?

▶ What popular athlete or movie star would probably be a great person to have lunch with and why?

> ▶ When it comes to the classroom seating assignments, is it better for the students to get to choose where they sit or is it better for the teacher to choose? Why?

THE GOOD NEWS AND THE BAD NEWS

Let's start with the good news: the baseline measurement may show a high likelihood of your students being able to demonstrate strong claim-making abilities. Indeed, chances are excellent that your kids will answer the prompt with a rock-solid statement that exemplifies real writing acumen. Of course, this is a direct result of your good work at the front of the room. Definitely a moment to pat yourself on the back.

Now the bad news: there might be a maddening lack of spillover. Sure, your students might compose wonderful claims but for some mystical reason, the subsequent sentences they compose afterward might NOT be highly reasonable, richly expressed, or well executed.

And this could very well make you want to pull your hair out!

Don't. Learning to write well is a recursive process whereby there is always going to be some inevitable backslide. That means when little Timmy says, "But I didn't know that the rules you mentioned about making a claim also needed to be applied to all the other sentences, too," your job is to just smile and repeat warm tropes like, "The joy of teaching, the joy of teaching, the joy of teaching."

Establish your next baseline measurement and know that Triple C Writing already has a plan in place for making sure the skills students have already learned in one area of short-response writing will transfer over to all other areas as well.

ACTION STEP 2: Define What It Means to Cite It! (And Why It Is So Important)

The "it" in Cite It! stands for evidence. It's the offering of proof that helps people better decide whether they ought to agree or disagree with the position being asserted. Therefore, when we Cite It! we are offering proof that's intended to show why our way of thinking makes sense.

> **Student-friendly definition of what it means to Cite It:**
> When you cite evidence, you are providing proof that supports your claim.
>
> Remember, a claim is when someone says "this is true" about something—it's when a person puts forth an idea that something is an actual fact.
>
> When we cite evidence we're saying, "and here is how I know this is true"—it's when a person puts forth strong, supporting information that proves the claim being made is worth believing.

Be aware there's a chance that students might ask, "Why do we even need to cite evidence? Isn't a highly reasonable, richly expressed, well-written claim enough?"

The answer is both yes and no; it depends. After all, some claims make it easy to arrive at a reasonable decision about whether or not it's worth agreeing or disagreeing with the statement being presented.

For example:

> Babies shouldn't be allowed to stick their fingers in electrical sockets even if the main power line to the house has been turned off.

Most reasonable people wouldn't require that the above claim needs evidence to substantiate its validity—its debatability is not very high. However, things gets a bit more tricky when we start to see claims like these:

▶ I deserve a new computer.

▶ It's not fair that I have to clean up my sister's mess.

Perhaps the speaker does deserve a new computer. Or do they? Maybe it isn't fair that the speaker has to clean up his or her sister's mess, or maybe it is. For claims like these, we definitely need some reasons to accept them before we give them our support.

These reasons will be the evidence that gets cited. They are the proof that demonstrates, "You see, my claim is worth believing."

OUR BRAIN'S THREE-STEP THOUGHT PROCESS

When we hear a claim—even if it's rock-solid—we typically go through a three-step evaluation process.

1. We reflect on the claim (checking to see if we understand the meaning of the statement).

2. We weigh the claim (evaluating how the statement measures up against our existing beliefs).

3. We decide whether we want to support the claim (considering to what degree we agree or disagree with the statement).

Knowing how to properly cite relevant, strong, accurate evidence can often be the great difference maker as to whether or not a claim eventually wins support and carries the day.

Here's a way to show students how important citing evidence to support their claims can actually be:

Student Claim	Student Evidence
"I deserve a new computer."	"I really want one."

In the above example, it's easy to see how citing weak evidence directly translates into not gaining much support for the position being asserted. Yet . . .

Student Claim	Student Evidence
"I deserve a new computer."	"My old computer just died and I want to be able to produce the best possible homework I can for school so I can be well-prepared to succeed in class like all the other top students in my grade."

What a difference, huh?

Unfortunately, strong evidence doesn't automatically mean that an audience will be convinced that a claim deserves support. In the example above there are a host of possible reasons why the student might not actually deserve a new computer that haven't yet been illuminated. (Perhaps her old computer died because she got frustrated with it and threw it against a wall—for the third time this month!) But this example does illustrate the vast difference between how citing high-quality evidence versus low-quality evidence affects how we see a claim.

Here are a few more examples:

Citing Weak Evidence

Kid's Claim	Kid's Evidence
"It's not fair that I have to clean up my sister's mess."	"The reason it's not fair is because all I want to do right now is sit on the couch, watch television, and eat chocolate ice cream."

Citing Strong Evidence

Kid's Claim	Kid's Evidence
"It's not fair that I have to clean up my sister's mess."	"The reason it's not fair is because for the last three days I have cleaned up her mess every time I've been asked to do so without saying a word and since I didn't even play with all those toys in the first place, I shouldn't have to always be the one who puts them away."

Citing Weak Evidence

Kid's Claim	Kid's Evidence
"Mike's grandmother is a good cook."	"She's in the kitchen a lot."

Citing Strong Evidence

Kid's Claim	Kid's Evidence
"Mike's grandmother is a good cook."	"She owns one of the most popular restaurants in town and has won multiple awards for the dishes she creates."

Citing Weak Evidence

Teacher's Claim	Teacher's Evidence
"Math is important."	"The reason is because I am the teacher and I said so."

Mastering Short-Response Writing: Claim It! Cite It! Cement It! © 2016 by Alan Sitomer • Scholastic Inc. • scholastic.com/MSRWresources

Citing Strong Evidence

Teacher's Claim	Teacher's Evidence
"Math is important."	"The reason is because later in life you will have to use math quite often and people who are good at math have a higher chance of attaining success in life no matter what their ambition."

THE FOUR TYPES OF EVIDENCE

There are four basic types of evidence writers cite to support their claims: statistical evidence, expert opinions, supportive stories, and instances of comparison. Depending on the claim, some are more effective than others.

Statistical Evidence

Includes evidence based on facts or data that can be verified for accuracy.

Example:

CLAIM IT!   Playing too many video games is bad for a child's health.

CITE IT!   The latest health studies from Washington, DC show that kids who play more than two hours of video games per day have a 38% greater chance of being out of shape and at risk for health issues later in life.

WHY STATISTICAL EVIDENCE IS GOOD: Supporting claims with specific facts and data that can be verified for accuracy is often highly convincing.

WHAT TO WATCH OUT FOR: Statistical evidence can't always be taken at face value, as it doesn't always tell the whole story. For example, there could be other statistical evidence that the author failed to cite (such as a

New York study showing that diet is the most critical element to a child's health, not whether or not they play video games, and so on). Facts and data are great but *caveat emptor*, let the buyer beware.

· · · · · ·

Expert Opinions (a.k.a. Testimonials)

Includes evidence that a specialist in a particular area, an authority on a subject, offers as supporting proof of a claim's truthfulness.

Example:

CLAIM IT!   Playing too many video games is bad for a child's health.

CITE IT!   Dr. Mark Hopper, a researcher from the Center of Childhood Health, warns parents that when they allow their kids to play too many video games, the chances of young people suffering from poor physical fitness are greatly increased.

WHY EXPERT OPINION IS GOOD: People trust the opinion of experts because it can be reasonably presumed that experts are well-informed authorities on the subject. In other words, who better than an expert to "know"?

WHAT TO WATCH OUT FOR: 1) Experts can be wrong. For example, here's an "expert opinion" published in *The Quarterly Review* back in 1825, on why not to buy into the hype surrounding the possibilities of train travel: "What can be more palpably absurd than the prospect held out of locomotives traveling twice as fast as stagecoaches?" 2) Experts can also have their own agenda when they offer their insights. Here's an example from Darryl F. Zanuck, head of 20th Century Fox movie studio, in 1946, a man so successful at pleasing audiences with his media products that he was considered a living legend at the time he said these words: "Television won't be able to hold on to any market it captures after the first six months. People will soon get tired of staring at a plywood box every night."

· · · · · ·

Supportive Stories (Anecdotal Evidence)

Includes evidence offered by citing specific instances in order to draw general, broad-brushstroke conclusions. Sometimes this evidence is based on the stories of other people.

Example:

CLAIM IT!   Playing too many video games is bad for a child's health.

CITE IT!   Mike Hampton, the extremely out-of-shape 14-year-old kid who lives down the block from me, sits on the couch playing video games for three hours every day.

WHY IT'S GOOD: Regardless of our culture, socioeconomic status, or nationality, human beings across the planet are raised on stories. We like to hear them and when they connect with us—particularly on an emotional level—we can be more easily persuaded to buy into the truthfulness of an asserted claim.

WHAT TO WATCH OUT FOR: The story of one person—or a group of people—does not automatically mean it characterizes the story of everyone else. When unaccompanied by other types of evidence to reinforce a claim, supportive stories often make it seem as if it's logical to conclude that what happened in one specific instance will happen to everyone else in similar general circumstances . . . yet seldom is this the actual case.

· · · · · ·

Instances of Comparison (a.k.a. Analogical Evidence)

Includes evidence offered by saying that since one thing is like another thing all other similar things that are compared will be alike as well.

Example:

CLAIM IT!   Playing too many video games is bad for a child's health.

CITE IT!   Joey is a hardcore gamer who is extremely out of shape,

> Paul is a hardcore gamer who is extremely out of shape, and Mitchell is a hardcore gamer who is extremely out of shape.

WHY IT'S GOOD: Comparisons help people see relationships between different things, so by illuminating the patterns that connect specific circumstances, conclusions can be drawn that have a foundation based in logic. (If it walks like a duck and quacks like a duck . . . .)

WHAT TO WATCH OUT FOR: Similar to the weaknesses of supportive stories, the connection between a few people or incidents does not automatically mean this will be a dependable pattern that proves true for all other similar incidents. Essentially, it would be dangerous to accept inferences that the connections between a few things mean they stand up as truth for the connections between all similar things.

ACTION STEP 3: Demonstrate How to Cite It! (Front-of-Class Write-Aloud)

We are now going to model how to Cite It! for young writers by using the instructional strategy of teacher Write-Alouds, as we did for Claim It!

But hold the phone! Before moving on, it's time to introduce young writers to a wonderful pedagogical tool that will help them better see the forest for the trees when it comes to composing rock-solid short responses.

COLOR-CODING SHORT-RESPONSE WRITING

Each sentence in a well-written Triple C short response has a very specific job. Yet, with conventions such as subject-verb agreement, comma usage, descriptive vocabulary, and the capitalization of proper nouns playing an important role, it's easy for young writers to lose track of making sure that each sentence says what it needs to say. This is why color-coding is such a wonderful strategy to raise achievement.

Color-coding also allows developing writers to literally see the bigger purpose—and remain mindful of the intended meaning—behind each sentence as it is being written.

Claim It! = BLUE

Cite it! = GREEN

Going forward, when students write in blue, they will know that the job of the sentence is to assert a claim (that is highly reasonable, richly expressed, and well-written). When they write in green, they will know that the job of the sentence is to cite support for the claim with evidence (that is relevant, strong, and accurate). In the next chapter, we learn about how to cement the evidence to the claim to create a rock-solid short response. Students will use orange for that step.

Why wait until now to introduce the idea of color-coding? Because up until this point, we have only been working with single sentences. Now that we are working with more than one sentence—and each sentence has a different job—the strategy of color-coding will make sense to young writers.

> Well-written paragraphs are, by default, well-organized paragraphs. Color-coding is a way of reinforcing for students that each sentence has a specific job; color-coding allows writers to remain constantly aware of the intent behind each of their sentences.

DRAFTING YOUR "WRITE-ALOUD" CITE IT! IN FRONT OF STUDENTS

Being that Triple C Writing scaffolds instruction and builds upon prior success, it makes sense to use claims from our previous Write-Alouds (see Chapter 4) as the starting point for the activities we are going to use to show students how to effectively support their claims. By tapping their prior knowledge (they have already seen/written these claims), it makes it easier for them to focus their attention on the art of citing evidence.

Below are some teacher Write-Alouds you might want to try. (Note that there are a few errors in some. This is so that we have source material for making editorial revisions during Action Step 5).

Claim It!	Cite It!
If we paint these walls green, it will help students feel more comfortable.	According to a new study, the color green ranks nineteen % higher than any other color choice for classroom walls because of greens connection with nature.
Students eat too much pizza.	According to Dr. Joel Hammer, kids between the ages of 8-fourteen are eating pizza an average of 3x per week.
Pretzels are the best snack ever invented.	Sally served pretzels at her birthday party, her halloween party, and her memorial day party and by the time each party ended, all of the pretzels had been like devoured by her guests.
Dolphins are cuter than kittens.	I think dolphins are cuter, my sis thinks dolphins are cuter, and my two best freinds think dolphins are way totally cuter than kittens.

Now that you have color-coded Claim It! in blue and Cite It! in green and done a few Write-Alouds for the sake of modeling how to support a claim by citing evidence, it's time to hand the steering wheel over to the students.

ACTION STEP 4: Task Students With Citing Evidence to Support Their Claim

You can have students call and respond, you can have students independently cite evidence to support their claims, you can break your class into collaborative learning groups and have each team of students cite a piece of evidence to support a claim, and so on. Choose the method that you feel will best serve your kids. (And know that there will be plenty of independent practice forthcoming so you don't need to worry about "not writing enough" if you choose to do, say, call-and-respond or group work right now.)

After students have selected a claim they have already written, lay out the nonnegotiable aspects of the current task being assigned:

Claim It! in blue

Claims need to be:

- ▶ Highly Reasonable

- ▶ Richly Expressed

- ▶ Well-Written

Cite It! in green

The evidence being cited must put forth supporting information that proves the claim being made is worth believing.

ACTION STEP 5: Demonstrate How to Revise a Citation of Evidence

It's time to revise your Cite It! statements in front of all your students. Once again, the reason is to show off the power of—and critical need for—revision.

In Chapter 4, we pounded the drum that "Writers constantly rewrite." In Chapter 5, we are marching to the beat of this same drummer.

Sometimes we revise for the sake of correcting errors and sometimes in order to revise our ideas so that they are strong, well considered, and well organized. I encourage teachers to tackle each aim individually and model the rewriting process step by step.

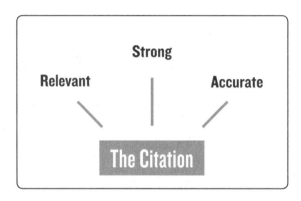

OBJECTIVE: Clean up spelling and grammatical errors in our Cite It! work.

CLAIM IT!   If we paint these walls green, it will help students feel more comfortable.

CITE IT!   According to a new study, the color green ranks ~~nineteen~~ 19% higher than any other color choice for classroom walls because of ~~greens~~ green's connection with nature.

CLAIM IT!   Students eat too much pizza.

CITE IT!   According to Dr. Joel Hammer, kids between the ages of ~~8 fourteen~~ 8–14 are eating pizza an average of ~~3 x~~ 3 times per week.

CLAIM IT!   Pretzels are the best snack ever invented.

CITE IT!   Sally served pretzels at her birthday party, her ~~halloween~~ Halloween party, and her ~~memorial day~~ Memorial Day party

and by the time each party ended, all of the pretzels had
been ~~like~~ devoured by her guests.

CLAIM IT!   Dolphins are cuter than kittens.

CITE IT!   I think dolphins are cuter, my ~~sis~~ sister thinks dolphins are
cuter, and my two best ~~freinds~~ friends think dolphins are ~~way
totally~~ cuter than kittens.

LOOKING AT THE FOUR TYPES OF EVIDENCE

In the Cite It! models provided, we used an example of Statistical Evidence,
Expert Opinions, Supportive Stories, and Instances of Comparison—in
that order. We did this because it offers teachers an opportunity to start
winnowing down the types of evidence students are encouraged to use.
Why should we become more selective at this point of the instructional
process? Because Supportive Stories and Instances of Comparison, while
types of evidence that offer some degree of credibility, don't have the
strength that Statistical Evidence and Expert Opinions do when it comes
to composing expository or argumentative short responses.

Taking a deep look at the four different types of evidence during your
second Write-Aloud allows you to show which type of evidence is the
strongest (more supportive) and which is the weakest (least convincing).

Really start to push your students' critical thinking skills by engaging
them in conversation about which type of evidence is most effective and
why as you do your front-of-class rewrite.

Statistical Evidence

CLAIM IT!   If we paint these walls green, it will help students feel
more comfortable.

CITE IT!   According to a new study, the color green ranks 19% higher
than any other color choice for classroom walls because of
green's connection with nature.

Expert Opinions

CLAIM IT!   Students eat too much pizza.

CITE IT!   According to Dr. Joel Hammer, kids between the ages of 8–14 are eating pizza an average of 3 times per week.

. . . . . .

Supportive Stories

CLAIM IT!   Pretzels are the best snack ever invented.

CITE IT!   Sally served pretzels at her birthday party, her Halloween party, and her Memorial Day party and by the time each party ended, all of the pretzels had been devoured by her guests.

. . . . . .

Instances of Comparison

CLAIM IT!   Dolphins are cuter than kittens.

CITE IT!   I think dolphins are cuter, my ~~sis~~ sister thinks dolphins are cuter, and my two best friends think dolphins are cuter than kittens.

It's not going to take long for students to see the high value of Statistical Evidence and Expert Opinions. Nor will it take them long to see how Supportive Stories and Instances of Comparison don't really do the job writers need when composing a rock-solid expository or argumentative short response.

Thus, for the next student rewrite, start encouraging students to use either Statistical Evidence and/or Expert Opinions to support their expository or argumentative claims.

THE DIFFERENCES BETWEEN OPINION WRITING, PERSUASIVE WRITING, AND ARGUMENTATIVE WRITING

If you're saying to yourself, "But not all claims can be—or need to be—supported with statistical evidence or expert opinions in order to be highly convincing," you are entirely correct. Sometimes supportive stories or instances of comparison are the most effective evidence to cite in order to buoy up a claim.

But not when it comes to Expository or Argumentative Writing. For Opinion Writing or Persuasive Writing, it's true that other forms of evidence might actually prove to be more effective.

To backtrack for a moment, we know that expository writing aims to explain, describe, or inform. Neutrality rules. Expository short responses tell us how or why in an unbiased manner.

On the other hand, argumentative writing aims to convince or sway. It's biased and subjective and tells an audience what to believe as truth by asserting a judgment.

Argumentative short-response writing relies heavily on evidence based in logical reasoning that is substantiated by data, facts, and statistics. Opinion short-response writing, on the other hand, relies primarily on evidence that is based on personal feelings or individual preferences. Persuasive short-response writing, to round it out, relies on evidence that best appeals to an audience's emotions.

This chart highlights the distinctions between all three:

	Argumentative	Opinion	Persuasive
Point of this type of writing	Get the reader to accept the asserted perspective as truth.	Share a personal preference or individual point of view.	Convince a reader to agree with an asserted position because it is the "right" position on the issue to embrace.
General tone of the writing	This is the truth and logical reasoning dictates it's the most prudent perspective to embrace.	This is what I personally believe and this is why I personally believe it.	The idea I am asserting is "right" and my passionate belief will stir your emotions so that you will believe it's "right" as well.
Most common type of evidence that will be provided	Statistics, facts, data and expert opinions	Personal feelings and individual opinions	Emotional appeals that blend personal feelings with facts; whatever will best emotionally resonate
Example:	When hosting a birthday party for the entire class, moms should always buy vanilla ice cream. According to studies done by the Ice Cream Industry of America, vanilla ice cream ranks as the number one most popular flavor for kids under the age of 18.	I think my mom should buy vanilla ice cream for my birthday party next week. Since I am the birthday girl and vanilla is my favorite flavor, I think I ought to be the one who gets to choose.	If you are a mom who is going to host a kid's birthday party, you should serve the guests vanilla ice cream. Vanilla is the tastiest flavor, vanilla is the most popular flavor, and vanilla is the flavor that best pairs up with whatever flavor birthday cake you decide to scoop it onto.

 Mastering Short-Response Writing: Claim It! Cite It! Cement It! © 2016 by Alan Sitomer • Scholastic Inc. • scholastic.com/MSRWresources

TIME OUT FOR SOME GRAMMAR, USAGE, OR SPELLING MINI-LESSONS

Triple C Writing offers many opportunities for inserting needed mini-lessons that focus on targeted writing standards where teachers see recurring grammatical, usage, and/or spelling errors. For example, perhaps your students are still struggling with apostrophes and possessives. Now would be a great time to more deeply dive into how and why you revised the apostrophe used in the model Cite It! sentences we just provided.

MODEL SENTENCE: According to a new study, the color green ranks 19% higher than any other color choice for classroom walls because of green's connection with nature.

GRAMMAR OPPORTUNITY: Explain why an apostrophe is needed for "green's connection."

EXPLANATION: The apostrophe has three, and only three, uses:

1. To show possession

   For example:

   - The lady's hat
   - Sandra's pencil
   - The teacher's water bottle

2. To indicate the omission of letters or numbers

   For example:

   - Jazz music was born in the '20s.
   - The students don't know the answer.
   - Every member of the class of '14 went to college.

3. To form plurals of lowercase letters

   For example:

   - Mind your p's and q's.
   - The word *banana* is spelled with three *a*'s.
   - The city Oconomowoc, WI, uses five *o*'s to spell its name.

Grammar-based mini-lessons—teaching opportunities that exist in the spaces between other academic objectives—are wonderful opportunities to be seized. Hit the ones your students need as you see that they need them in order to refine grammar, usage, and spelling as you go.

ACTION STEP 6: Task Students With Revising Their Citation of Evidence

You can have students come to the front of the room and share a "before and after" for everyone to see, you can visit each of your collaborative groupings to see how kids evolved from A to B in their teams—the options for instruction are plentiful, and there is no "wrong" or "right" way to approach this part of the lesson.

WHERE DO THEY GET THE STATISTICAL EVIDENCE OR EXPERT OPINIONS? INCORPORATING SOURCE TEXT

As mentioned previously, Triple C Writing is steeped in tapping the power of the reading/writing connection. To that end, if students' hands suddenly start flying into the air asking, "But where do I get statistical evidence or expert opinions to support my claim?" the perfect door has been opened to tell students, "You do research."

Well-informed expository or argumentative claims state what you know and how you know it. This means it's time to bring source text into the mix. Here is a quick guide on how students can assess the credibility of source text in print form. The University of California at Santa Cruz provides these insights on how to evaluate the quality and credibility of your sources:

Not all information is created equal. Just because you find information at the library does not guarantee that it is accurate or good research. In an academic setting, being able to critically evaluate information is necessary in order to conduct quality research. Each item you find must be evaluated to determine its quality and credibility in order to best support your research.

To evaluate a source, consider the following:

Authority

▶ Who published the source? Is it a university press or a large reputable publisher? Is it from a government agency? Is the source self-published? What is the purpose of the publication?

▶ Where does the information in the source come from? Does the information appear to be valid and well-researched, or is it questionable and unsupported by evidence? Is there a list of references or works cited? What is the quality of these references?

▶ Who is the author? What are the author's credentials (educational background, past writing, experience) in this area? Have you seen the author's name cited in other sources or bibliographies?

▶ Is the content a firsthand account or is it being retold? Primary sources are the raw material of the research process; secondary sources are based on primary sources.

Currency

▶ When was the source published? Is the source current or out of date for your topic?

Purpose

▶ What is the author's intention? Is the information fact, opinion, or propaganda? Is the author's point of view objective and impartial? Is the language free of emotion-rousing words or bias?

▶ Is the publication organized logically? Are the main points clearly presented? Do you find the text easy to read? Is the author repetitive?

Source: University of California Santa Cruz University Library, http://library.ucsc.edu/help/research/evaluate-the-quality-and-credibility-of-your-sources

The University of California at Santa Cruz also provides insights on how students can evaluate material they find on the Internet:

Unlike the library's collection of online databases, information retrieved using search engines (such as Google) has not been evaluated and/or organized by librarians, or humans for that matter. Anyone can publish on the Web without passing the content through an editor. Pages might be written by an expert on the topic, a journalist, a disgruntled consumer, or even a child. There are no standards to ensure accuracy. Web resources are not permanent. Some well-maintained sites are updated with very current information, but other sites may become quickly dated or disappear altogether without much, if any, notice.

Using an Internet Source in Your Research

If you are using a web page as a possible research citation, you should consider the following criteria:

Authority

It is often difficult to determine who the author or sponsor of a web page is, much less their credentials or qualifications.

▶ Is the author identified? If so, are his/her credentials/ qualifications listed?

▶ Does the web page have a sponsor? If so, is the sponsor reputable?

▶ Does the web page provide information about the author or the sponsor? Is there contact information for the author? (e.g., email address, mailing address, phone number)?

▶ Does the URL contain a .edu or .gov domain (e.g., http://library.ucsc.edu)?

Purpose

It is important to determine the goals of the web page. You can check to see if these are clearly stated in a mission statement or an "About Us" page. This can help you determine if the page is intended to inform, explain, or persuade.

▶ What is the purpose or motive for the site (e.g., educational, commercial, entertainment, promotional)?

▶ Is the information biased or is the author presenting more than one side of the argument?

▶ Is the page designed to sway opinion? Is the purpose of the page clearly identified?

▶ Is there a sponsor or advertising on the page? If so, does this influence the information? Is the site trying to sell you something? How easy is it to differentiate advertisement from content?

Currency

The effectiveness of a web page can sometime be lessened if it becomes out of date. If the web page relies on information such as hyperlinks, directory, or timely information, etc., it should be updated and revised as the information changes.

▶ Are dates provided for when the information was written or when the page was last modified or updated?

▶ Are the links (if any) up to date?

Coverage

Web resources are often presented in a different context from print resources, making it difficult to determine the extent of coverage.

▶ What topics are covered?

▶ How in depth does the information go?

▶ Does the page offer information not found elsewhere?

Source: University of California Santa Cruz University Library, http://library.ucsc.edu/help/research/evaluate-content-from-the-web

Citing Evidence Using Three Different Lenses

It's now time for students to start individually citing evidence to support their claims. As before, we'll read and evaluate evidence through a set of three different lenses before tasking students with writing their own Cite It! assignments.

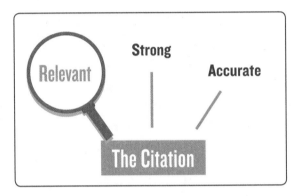

Read the following claim and have students score it (3, 2, or 1) in each of the following three categories:

Making sure that schools serve their students healthy, delicious food for lunch stands out as an important issue for parents. According to research published by the National School Lunch Program, schools reported that students had eaten more fruits and vegetables, had longer attention spans, and had fewer behavior problems when they were served tasty, nutritious meal options.

RELEVANT: In terms of how relevant the evidence is . . .

> ▶ 3 points if the evidence clearly and directly supports the claim
>
> ▶ 2 points if the evidence somewhat directly supports the claim
>
> ▶ 1 point if the evidence only slightly supports the claim

MY SCORE: _____

STRONG: In terms of how strong the writer's evidence is . . .

> ▶ 3 points if the evidence is logical, convincing, and solid
>
> ▶ 2 points if the evidence has some merit but still feels as if it could be improved
>
> ▶ 1 point if the evidence weakly supports the claim and needs much more gusto

MY SCORE: _____

ACCURATE: In terms of how precise and truthful the evidence is . . .

> ▶ 3 points if the evidence is truthful and based in research that can be verified
>
> ▶ 2 points if the evidence appears truthful and valid but is not specific with references that are clearly defined
>
> ▶ 1 point if the evidence might or might not be truthful and/or there is no way or doing further research to verify the support being offered

MY SCORE: _____

BONUS: Does this claim have a certain special something, that little extra piece of strength and quality that makes it deserving of a bonus point? (Add 1 point if the answer is yes.)

BONUS POINT: _____   GRAND TOTAL: _____

Follow the same procedure with the following samples:

▶ Yellow dogs are smarter than white dogs. Three of my neighbors have yellow dogs and all of them are much more intelligent than my white dog.

▶ Hot dogs should always be topped with either ketchup or mustard. As the author of the online article "How to Properly Eat a Hot Dog" states, "People who do not put either of these condiments on their hot dogs are making a big mistake."

▶ Reading about monsters is more enjoyable than reading about rabbits. Scary monsters make boys smile.

What Does It Mean to Cite Relevant Evidence?

Before asking students to provide highly relevant support for their claims, define for them what the task means.

> Relevant evidence directly supports the central idea being stated by the claim; it is fitting, to the point, and "on the button."

Example:

Relevant Citation of Supportive Evidence	Irrelevant Citation of Supportive Evidence
The school should offer students time each day to relax, play, and reenergize. Dr. Tim Marky, a child psychologist from Reynolds University, says that kids must have time to simply be kids.	The school should offer students time each day to relax, play, and reenergize. Dr. Tim Marky, a child psychologist from Reynolds University, says that only a bad principal wouldn't want kids to get a good night's sleep, too.

Relevant Citation of Supportive Evidence	Irrelevant Citation of Supportive Evidence
Teachers ought to expect that parents will sometimes help their kids with homework. A new study from Chaplin College has found that 81% of parents assist with homework at least once a week.	Teachers ought to expect that parents will sometimes help their kids with homework. A new study from Chaplin College has also found that teachers should give their students less homework.

Ask students to make a claim and cite one piece of relevant evidence to support their claim about . . .

- ▶ the most popular type of vacation for a family to take.

- ▶ the best type of shoes to wear for playing basketball.

- ▶ the importance of being a well-organized student.

In terms of how relevant the evidence is, ask students to give themselves a score, from 1 to 3:

- ▶ 3 points if the evidence clearly and directly supports the claim

- ▶ 2 points if the evidence somewhat directly supports the claim

- ▶ 1 point if the evidence only slightly supports the claim

GATEKEEPING CHECKPOINT: Though only three examples have been provided, you might want to assign as many as 20 different tasks. Continue to assign the "make a claim and provide one piece of relevant evidence" assignment until you feel your students are rock-solid and ready to move on.

WHAT DOES IT MEAN TO CITE STRONG EVIDENCE?

Before asking students to cite strong evidence to support their claims, define for them what the task means.

> Strong evidence provides solid proof that a claim is worth believing; it backs up a claim with direct logic, solid facts, data, quotes, expert opinions, and/or authority that can be directly tied to the statement being asserted.

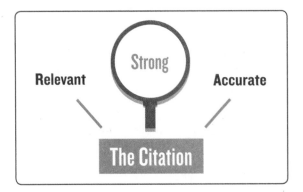

Example:

Relevant Citation of Supportive Evidence	Irrelevant Citation of Supportive Evidence
It's critical that teachers send the clear message that bullying will not be tolerated at school. The U.S. Department of Health and Human Services says that students who are bullied can suffer from depression, anxiety, and low academic performance.	It's critical that teachers send the clear message that bullying will not be tolerated at school. The U.S. Department of Health and Human Services thinks teaching is an important and rewarding job.

Relevant Citation of Supportive Evidence	Irrelevant Citation of Supportive Evidence
Serving vanilla-and-chocolate-swirl-flavored ice cream cake adds an extra dash of awesomeness to a kid's birthday party. A surprising new survey shows that 8 out of 10 kids say they have more fun at birthday parties when swirled ice cream cake is served.	Serving vanilla-and-chocolate-swirl-flavored ice cream cake adds an extra dash of awesomeness to a kid's birthday party. A surprising new survey shows that kids also like magicians to perform at birthday parties, too.

Ask students to make a claim and provide one piece of strong evidence about . . .

 ▶ the best breakfast to serve a six-year-old.

 ▶ the most fun game to play with a group of other friends.

 ▶ the worst thing about a rainy day.

In terms of how strong the evidence is, ask students to give themselves a score, from 1 to 3:

 ▶ 3 points if the evidence is logical, convincing, and solid

 ▶ 2 points if the evidence has some merit but still feels as if it could be improved

 ▶ 1 point if the evidence weakly supports the claim and needs much more gusto

GATEKEEPING CHECKPOINT: Though only three examples have been provided, you might want to assign as many as 20 different tasks. Continue to assign the "make a claim and provide one piece of strong evidence" assignment until you feel your students are rock-solid and ready to move on.

WHAT DOES IT MEAN TO CITE ACCURATE EVIDENCE?

Before asking students to cite accurate evidence to support their claims, define for them what the task means.

> Accurate evidence is supportive proof that can be double-checked and verified for truthfulness (information, quotes, statistics), and must be used in context and always strive to capture the true intent of what the original speaker intended.

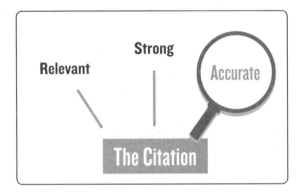

Example:

Accurate Claim	Inaccurate Claim
Doctors agree that eating too much candy is detrimental to a child's health. While Dr. Sarah Polley does say that some candy is okay, her expert opinion is that serving sweets ought to be rare and certainly not every day.	Doctors agree that eating too much candy is detrimental to a child's health. However, Dr. Sarah Polley is an expert on the subject and she says that eating candy is okay so there is nothing to be too worried about.

Accurate Claim	Inaccurate Claim
Sleepover parties can be fun but usually a kid doesn't get too much sleep. This is a problem because sleep studies by the National Sleep Foundation show that young people need 60% more rest than what they normally get at overnight parties.	Sleepover parties can be fun but usually a kid doesn't get too much sleep. This is not a problem, though, because sleep studies by the National Sleep Foundation show that young people get at least 40% of the rest that they'd normally get at overnight parties.

Ask students to make a claim and provide one piece of accurate evidence about . . .

- ▶ the worst thing to give a kid for a birthday present.
- ▶ the scariest character ever to appear in a movie.
- ▶ what pets can teach people about relationships.

For each claim, ask students to give themselves a score, from 1 to 3:

- ▶ 3 points if the evidence is truthful and based in research that can be verified
- ▶ 2 points if the evidence appears truthful and valid but is not specific with references that are clearly defined
- ▶ 1 point if the evidence might or might not be truthful and/or there is no way or doing further research to verify the support being offered

GATEKEEPING CHECKPOINT: Though only three examples have been provided, you might want to assign as many as 20 different claims. Continue to assign the "Make a claim and provide accurate evidence" task until you feel your students are rock-solid and ready to move on.

Students Craft Relevant, Strong, Accurate Evidence to Support Their Claims

Wowz-a-doozy! Look at how far we've come. Triple C Writing is at the point of having students deliver a mere two sentences, but when the lion's share of your students can deliver two rock-solid sentences that embody all the qualities we've been working on, that is a HUGE win!

And quite frankly, I am not sure that a lot of our nation's college graduates could currently execute this task (a point that speaks to the value of smart instruction more than the intelligence of the writer).

Though our work to this point might have felt a bit slow and dense, these roots are deep and the skills we have built will travel with students as they move through elementary school, into middle school, and on to high school, college, and beyond.

Triple C Writing opens a world of possible.

However, let's not count our chickens before they are hatched. It's now time for students to refine their skills in each of the domains we've been working on and put it all together. Of course, this is also the moment when we now "cross swim lanes" and comment on apostrophe usage, relevant evidence, the reasonableness of a claim, the accuracy of the citation, and so on, without letting any of these six areas "slide."

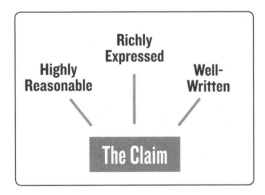

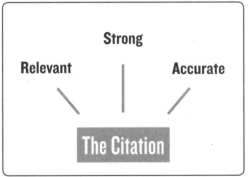

Having parsed out all the ingredients, it's now time for kids to put a whole meal together. Any conversation about any skills we have covered in any part of the work is fair game.

Tips for Elevating Performance

Here are a few tips to share with your students—as well as a few pitfalls to consciously avoid—that will empower your kids to Cite It! by providing rock-solid evidence.

Please note that the following offers materials that top professional writers use all the time in the "real" world. It's not cheating to provide precise instructions on how to quote from a source text or to offer students clear-cut sentence starters. No one accuses a plumber of "cheating" when he uses a wrench to fasten a screw as opposed to using his fingers. What follows are simply the "tools of the trade."

THREE WAYS TO CITE IT!

Quote it

Quoting is a great way of including information, ideas, and insights from various outside sources into your evidence in order to build its credibility and strength.

Specifically, a quote uses the exact words of an author, extracted literally word for word from outside material.

Yes, as long as credit is properly accorded, quoting another person's words exactly as they were once presented is entirely okay. This is why quoting often uses quotation marks as a grammatical signal to indicate that the material inside the quotation marks is the precise words of someone else as taken from another source.

Tips on when to use quotations. Quote it if:

> ▶ the expertise offered by the quote directly backs up your claim.

- the quoted words provide particularly excellent or appropriate support or proof.

- your claim takes a position that relies on the reader understanding exactly what another person says about the topic.

Paraphrase it

Paraphrasing is when a writer takes a specific section of text and puts it into her own words. Put another way, it's when a writer recasts ideas or information from a source in her own unique, different way—while, of course, mentioning the source.

Most important about paraphrasing is that a writer does not use the original wording from the source; the writer says the same basic thing but in their own unique way. (Using the original wording from a source is either quoting or plagarism.)

Tip on when to using paraphrasing. You might want to paraphrase if:

- you want to provide strong evidence but the original words aren't dynamic enough to quote.

- you are presenting information or ideas that are unlikely to be questioned.

- you seek to support your claim with an especially relevant point in the source material.

Summarize it

Summarizing offers a big-picture overview of source material. While paraphrasing often focuses on a specific, usually short bit of text (like a sentence, phrase, or paragraph), summaries—you guessed it—sum it all up. They take longer chunks of information and ideas (lengthy text, multiple source materials, or entire bodies of content) and boil it all down into a concise, general synopsis.

Summaries can be valuable when a writer seeks to incorporate a large number of sources or ideas; however, when it comes to citing relevant, strong, accurate evidence, summarization is often the least effective way of providing support for a claim in short-response writing.

It's rare that this strategy would be chosen before quoting or paraphrasing as the most preferable means of supporting a claim because summaries are, by their very nature, vague. Thus, we've not included any tips because we want to slant our students toward more exactness.

For Example:

REPORT

Bullying is a serious public health problem

WASHINGTON (AP)—Zero-tolerance policies are ineffective in combating bullying, an independent government advisory group says, in urging schools to take a more preventative approach that includes teaching tolerance to address this "serious public health problem."

In a report released Tuesday, the National Academies of Sciences, Engineering, and Medicine said bullying should no longer be dismissed as merely a matter of kids being kids. "Its prevalence perpetuates its normalization. But bullying is not a normal part of childhood," the report said.

Schools, the researchers concluded, should end zero-tolerance policies that automatically suspend students for bullying.

"There's no evidence that they are impactful in a positive way," said Catherine Bradshaw, a professor and associate dean at the University of Virginia, and part of the committee that wrote the report. "They can actually do more harm than good and in fact don't provide the skill training or replacement behaviors for youth that are suspended or expelled."

The report also said zero-tolerance policies may lead to an underreporting of bullying because suspensions are perceived as too punitive.

Frederick Rivara, chairman of the committee and a professor of pediatrics and epidemiology at the University of Washington, cautioned that bullying has lasting negative consequences and cannot be ignored. "While there is not a quick fix or one-size-fits-all solution, the evidence clearly supports preventive and interventional policy and practice," he said.

Quote it *example*:

Schools have to reconsider how they discipline students for bullying. As Catherine Bradshaw, a professor and associate dean at the University of Virginia, says, some policies "can actually do more harm than good."

Paraphrase it *example*:

Schools have to reconsider how they discipline students for bullying. Professor Catherine Bradshaw believes current policies are actually hurting students instead of helping them.

Summarize it *example*:

Schools have to reconsider how they discipline students for bullying. University professors think we need to change our prevention policies.

PROVIDE SENTENCE STARTERS

Students have to gain academic language proficiency in order to become rock-solid short-response writers. As they learn to do so, there is no need for young writers to reinvent the wheel. Sentence starters provide a partial frame for Cite It! evidence but they leave it up to the writer to complete the idea on his or her own.

Sentence starters are helpful because they often provide a structure that exceeds what young writers would typically be able to create on their own. Of course, as time goes on, students acquire the structure much like students acquire advanced vocabulary: at first it's a bit clunky and somewhat challenging but after repeated exposure the notions are infused into students' lexicons.

Here are a few sentence starters to Cite It! that set the table for a rock-solid short response:

From Source Text

According to the text _____ .

The author stated _____ .

The picture shows _____ .

The writer mentioned _____ .

On page _____ it said _____ .

The graphic supports this claim because _____ .

The text explicitly states _____ .

My evidence to support this claim is based on _____ .

From Non-Source Text

I think _____ because _____ .

One example that supports my belief is _____ .

Evidence from _____ shows that _____ .

The reason I believe _____ is because _____ .

I feel _____ as a result of _____ .

Mastering Short-Response Writing: Claim It! Cite It! Cement It! © 2016 by Alan Sitomer • Scholastic Inc. • scholastic.com/MSRWresources

Moving On to the Third C: Cement It!

We're now back at the proverbial fork in the road. Do you feel as if your students own the ability to cite relevant, strong, accurate evidence to support their claims? Or do you think that your students still need more deliberate practice? As always, you're the teacher and no one other than you is best suited to make the call as to whether it's time to move on. There's no artificial clock kids are racing against so if your students need a little more time, grant them the space they need.

Moving on? *Congrats*! Well done. Need to circle back for a little more fine-tuning? *Congrats* as well!

CHAPTER 6

The Third C:
Cement It!

The claim has been made and the evidence has been cited but there's one more critical thing writers must do in order to compose a rock-solid short response.

That's right, it's time to wrap this baby up with a well-reasoned conclusion. Other types of extended forms of composition afford writers the luxury of reasserting positions, mustering up additional evidence, asserting counterclaims, rebutting contentions, and so on. With short-response writing, however, brevity is your best friend. In the interest of being concise, we want to finalize our ideas, drive home the reasoning that underpins our original claim, and then exit stage left.

To sum up: we state our claim, we support our claim with evidence, and then we cement our claim with a rock-solid conclusion.

Claim It! ⟶ Says what you know

Cite It! ⟶ Says how you know it

Cement It! ⟶ Says why you know it

Your claim is something you think is true, your evidence is the proof that your thinking makes sense, and your conclusion contains logical reasoning to connect your evidence to your claim in a convincing and decisive manner.

The Instructional Action Steps

ACTION STEP **1** ▶ **DETERMINE** Where Your Students Are (Baseline Measurement)

ACTION STEP **2** ▶ **DEFINE** What It Means to Cement It! (And Why It Is So Important)

ACTION STEP **3** ▶ **DEMONSTRATE** How to Cement It! (Front-of-Class Write-Aloud)

ACTION STEP **4** ▶ **TASK** Students With Cementing Their Short Response

ACTION STEP **5** ▶ **DEMONSTRATE** How to Revise a Cement It! Conclusion

ACTION STEP **6** ▶ **TASK** Students With Revising Their Cement It! Conclusions

ACTION STEP 1: Determine Where Your Students Are (Baseline Measurement)

It stands to reason that the Third C (Cement it!) will follow the same series of Instructional Action Steps as the previous two Cs (Claim It! and Cite It!). This means we'll once again begin by obtaining a baseline measurement of students' current abilities.

Here are a few sample prompts you may want to assign. (As previously mentioned, try not offer any directives about quality, length of response, grammar, and so on; let's just see where our young writers are):

Using at least one piece of evidence to support your response, please answer the following questions:

▶ What is the most feared creature in nature and why?

▶ If you could choose one character to leap out of a book and literally come to life, who would it be and why?

▶ Would it be better or worse for students in elementary school if we extended the school day by an additional two hours each afternoon so kids could spend more time in class? Explain why or why not.

WHAT YOU MIGHT OR MIGHT NOT SEE

Fasten your seatbelts because by this point you might actually start to see properly punctuated sentences complementing strongly asserted claims that have been supported by effective and well-considered evidence.

Hooray!

Also, you might not. (Sad face.)

As the French might say, *c'est la vie.*

Indeed, with some students it still might be "one step forward and two steps back" and with others it might be "one step forward followed by another step forward followed by yet another step forward" with hardly any backslide.

Just keep working the process. Triple C Writing is not finished yet, which means that your students are still going to find themselves somewhere on a continuum of achievement. Perhaps you'll discover that a great many of your young writers don't even offer a conclusion after you assign this baseline measurement because they believe the evidence they cited speaks for itself. On the other hand, you also might discover that some

Mastering Short-Response Writing: Claim It! Cite It! Cement It! © 2016 by Alan Sitomer • Scholastic Inc. • scholastic.com/MSRWresources

kids go on and on and on, offering citation after citation after citation to support their claim as if evidentiary volume equates to expository or argumentative effectiveness.

No need to hit the panic button; just attain a baseline measurement of where your young writers are, knowing that we're now headed for the home stretch where we'll work hard to iron out the remaining wrinkles.

ACTION STEP 2: Define What It Means to Cement It! (And Why It Is So Important)

Cement is a binder. It's quite literally a substance that sets and hardens and "unites," "glues," or "connects" materials.

Of course, most students probably know the word *cement* as a noun, as a thing.

> "Joey made handprints in the wet cement."
>
> "When Cindy dropped an egg on the hard cement, it exploded."

In Triple C Writing, however, we are using the word *cement* as a verb, as an action.

> "If we cement enough bricks together, we can build a house."
>
> "A bride and groom cement their relationship by kissing after they exchange wedding vows."

BUT WHAT ARE WE CEMENTING?

The "it" in Cement It! stands for the entirety of the short response we have composed up until this point. In other words, we are about to cement the claim and the evidence together.

How? Through the logical reasoning of a strongly constructed—yet concise—conclusion.

> **Student-friendly definition of what it means to Cement It:**
> When writers cement their evidence and their claim together with a strong, tight conclusion, they provide a logical reason why their claim makes good sense.

Of course, some students might ask, "Why do we need to Cement It! at all? Isn't a highly reasonable, richly expressed, well-written claim that is supported by relevant, strong, accurate evidence enough?"

There are two answers to this question. The first speaks directly to the reason why Triple C Writing includes a Cement It! statement.

Without explaining how evidence specifically supports a claim, writers leave it to the audience to infer it.

Sometimes this can work.

For example:

> It's not fair that I must clean up the messy kitchen floor.
> I didn't spill the milk.

At first blush, this evidence seems to infer a logical line of reasoning that makes good sense. In fact, without any additional information, a reader might be swayed enough by the claim and its support to not really require more information for the argument being presented.

Yet sometimes the lack of direct reasoning baffles readers and leaves them scratching their heads.

Let's look at the same claim and support from a perspective of knowing that the writer's family dog, Lucky, spilled the milk when she jumped up on the counter (which she's not supposed to do).

> It's not fair that I must clean up the messy kitchen floor. I didn't spill the milk.

Suddenly, the new piece of information makes the claim seem preposterous. After all, does the writer expect that the dog is going to clean up the messy floor? In this instance, the lack of direct reasoning binding the evidence to the claim makes all the difference in the world.

Yet, with a well-reasoned, presentable conclusion that ties the evidence to the claim, perceptions can change again. For example:

> It's not fair that I must clean up the messy kitchen floor. I didn't spill the milk. Of course, since Tommy brought the dog home in the first place and promised to be 100% responsible for it no matter what, it only makes sense that my brother gets his lazy butt off the couch and cleans up the mess instead of me.

No, I have never met Tommy, but that kid is going to have produce something Shakespearean or else he is soon going to be on his hands and knees sopping up the mutt's milky disaster.

The Writer's Rule of Three

The second reason why short-response writers need to CEMENT IT! stems from what's known as the Writer's Rule of Three.

The Rule of Three is a writing principle that says that presenting things in groups of three is more effective than any other numerical grouping choice. Threes are funnier, threes are more memorable, threes are scarier, and so on.

The thinking goes that having a group of three combines the power of brevity with the power of presenting a pattern with the power of establishing a rhythm while still allowing for either a twist or a "hammer it home" punctuation point.

The power of three can be simple, direct, and catchy while at the same time offer breadth, depth, and scope. (Notice the threes?) Examples abound everywhere:

- Stop, drop, and roll.
- Your beauty shines brighter than the sun, the moon, and the stars.
- Do you promise to tell the truth, the whole truth, and nothing but the truth?

No, the Rule of Three is not mandatory but rock-solid writers know that concepts or ideas presented in threes are inherently more interesting, enjoyable, or memorable.

ACTION STEP 3: Demonstrate How to Cement It! (Front-of-Class Write-Aloud)

Since each section of a well-written short response has its own specific job—and we know the value color coding can bring to advancing the skills of young writers—it's now time to break out a new hue.

CLAIM IT! = BLUE

CITE IT! = GREEN

CEMENT IT! = ORANGE

When students write in blue, they know that the job of the sentence is to assert a claim (that is highly reasonable, richly expressed, and well written). When they write in green, kids know that the job of the section is to cite support for the claim with evidence (that is relevant, strong, and accurate). We're now teaching students that when they write in orange, the job of their words is to wrap up their short response with a well-reasoned, presentable, concluding sentence.

DRAFTING YOUR "WRITE-ALOUD" CEMENT IT! IN FRONT OF STUDENTS

Once again, we're going to scaffold instruction and build upon prior success by using the claims and evidence from our previous Write-Alouds. By tapping students' prior knowledge—since they have already seen/ written these claims and evidence—it's easier for developing writers to focus their attention on the new skill we are introducing: cementing their short response. Therefore, lock in on the orange area right now and keep as much of the instruction contained in this section as possible.

Here are some teacher Write-Alouds you might want to incorporate. As before, there are a few errors in some of the Cement It! sentences below. This is so that we have source material for making revisions during Action Step 5. (Note that we've incorporated errors *only* in the orange section because we want to keep the students' attention on this part of the short response.)

CLAIM IT!   If we paint these walls green, it will help students feel more comfortable.

CITE IT!   According to a new study, the color green ranks 19% higher than any other color choice for classroom walls because of green's connection with nature.

CEMENT IT! Since students performs better in school when they feel most comfurtable, painting the Classroom walls green makes good sense.

. . . .

CLAIM IT! Students eat too much pizza.

CITE IT! According to Dr. Joel Hammer, kids between the ages of 8–14 are eating pizza an average of 3 times per week.

CEMENT IT! Because experts like dr. Hammer believe yung people need a a diet that includes a wide variety of foods, Students should eat less pizza.

. . . .

CLAIM IT! Teachers ought to expect that parents will sometimes help their kids with homework.

CITE IT! A new study from Chaplin College has found that 81% of parents assist with homework at least once a week.

CEMENT IT! With research showing that this many parent helps their children, teachers can't be supersurprised that students sometimes get help @ home.

. . . .

CLAIM IT! The school should offer students time each day to relax, play, and reenergize.

CITE IT! Dr. Tim Marky, a child psychologist from Reynolds University, says that kids must have time to simply be kids.

CEMENT IT! Of course, it makes sense that schools want what's best for they're students so when an expert says that kids need time two just be kids, schools ought to make tim each day for Young People to relax play and reenergize.

Make sure to point out how all of the orange sentences cement the short response by connecting the claim and the evidence. Since this is a new skill for many students, it might be a good idea to go back and review the synonyms for the word *cement*.

KEEPING IT SIMPLE: CEMENT IT! SENTENCE STARTERS

The Cement It! stage of Triple C Writing is, in some ways, the simplest C for students to compose. It also holds the potential to be the most formidable.

The simplicity stems from the fact that the answers are already right in front of a student writer's nose. Kids already have a claim, they already have the evidence, and they already (ought to, at least in their heads) have a logical reason why the evidence supports the claim. If they do, the last C can almost write itself.

The formidability of the last C comes from the fact that the logical reasoning required to compose a strong Cement It! sentence ascends high on the Richter scale of cognitive demand. Writing effective concluding sentences takes practice. For some students, scaffolding will be necessary in the form of sentence starters. Here are a few examples.

▶ Since the evidence says ____*(restate evidence)*_____, the idea that ___*(restate claim)*_____ is true.

▶ Therefore, it's clear that the ___*(claim)*_____ must be believed because ____*(the evidence)*_____ proves this is the case.

▶ With the data showing ____*(restate evidence)*_____, it's clear that ___*(restate claim)*_____ is correct.

▶ Because __*(expert opinion)*____ says _*(restate evidence)*____, my assertion that ___*(restate claim)*_____ makes good sense.

If you prefer to offer your students less detailed sentence starters that don't do as much of the heavy lifting for your writers, here are a few introductory words and/or phrases that rock-solid writers often turn to in order to pen concrete conclusions:

▶ To sum up _____.

▶ Since _____.

▶ Because _____.

▶ Given that _____.

▶ Seeing as _____.

▶ This shows _____.

▶ Of course _____.

▶ Therefore _____.

▶ All in all _____.

▶ In view of the fact that _____.

▶ Add it all up and this means _____.

Now that you have color-coded Claim It! in blue, Cite It! in green, and Cement It! in orange and modeled a few Write-Alouds, it's time to put the power of the pen back into the hands of your students.

ACTION STEP 4: Task Students With Cementing Their Conclusions

You can have students call and respond, you can have students independently compose conclusions, you can divide your class into collaborative learning groups and have each team craft an end sentence that connects the evidence to the claim, and so on. Choose the strategy you feel is most apropos to serving the needs of your learners.

> **TASK:** Have students follow the model by cementing a claim of their own.

In Chapter 5, we suggested students create a claim and cite evidence to support their assertion about anything from the quality of the food being served on campus to the importance of exercise. Encourage your young writers to start with one of those claims. Remind them of the following:

Claim It! in blue
Claims need to be:

- ▶ Highly Reasonable
- ▶ Richly Expressed
- ▶ Well-Written

Cite It! in green
Evidence needs to be:

- ▶ Relevant
- ▶ Strong
- ▶ Accurate

Cement It! in orange
A closing sentence that logically shows how the evidence supports the claim.

The guiding question writers must answer to determine whether or not they have written an effective Cement It! conclusion is this: Why does the evidence support the claim? (What's the reason?) To help your young writers along, there are a few more "tricks of the trade" to share.

THE THREE COMPONENTS OF A ROCK-SOLID CONCLUSION

1. The conclusion restates—not repeats, but restates—the claim.

2. The conclusion restates—not repeats, but restates—the evidence.

3. The conclusion cements the claim and the evidence together through a clear and direct line of logical reasoning.

BREAKING IT DOWN: A CEMENT IT! WRITE-ALOUD

It may help your students to talk about the process of composing a conclusion. Here is one possible way of talking through a Write-Aloud with your class.

Before I write my Cement It! conclusion, I have to remember the job this sentence will have in my short response. The goal of the words I am writing in orange is to answer the question, "Why does the evidence support the claim? (What's the reason?)"

To answer this question, I'll need to make sure I understand the claim. So I reread it.

> The school should offer students time each day to relax, play, and reenergize.

The claim says the school needs to offer students time each day to relax and play. I am sort of repeating it instead of restating it but for right now, that's okay. What most important is that I understand it.

Next, I need to make sure I understand the evidence that's been cited, so I reread that as well.

> Dr. Tim Marky, a child psychologist from Reynolds University, says that kids must have time to simply be kids.

The evidence cited is an expert opinion that says, "kids need time to just be kids." Good, I've got that as well. So, back to tackling the job of this sentence: how does the evidence support the claim?

At this point, I am just going to try to get my ideas together. I don't even have to write them down—I can merely think it out for now. Plus, I know if I do write it down, I can rewrite it later.

My answer goes something like this: the evidence supports the claim because when the child psychologist says "kids need time to just be kids," he is agreeing with the fact that schools need to offer students time each day away from their schoolwork to relax, play and reenergize if schools really want to do what's best for their students.

Great. I have an answer. The logic makes sense but I know it's still a little long. I know that crafting the answer into one solid sentence is going to take a bit of work but I can feel happy about the fact that my thinking makes sense; that's what is most important right now.

The best place for me to now turn is to my writer's toolbox. Many other writers have written strong Cement It! sentences in the past and I know I have a few sentence starters I can use in order to set myself up for success.

Time to be smart and follow the road map that has already been charted for me.

First, I know there are three parts I want to include in this one sentence. I also know that the order in which I present these three parts does not matter.

Wow, three things in one sentence. I have to admit, that makes me a bit nervous. I am not sure if I'll be able to do all of this. However, I need to remember I have tools at my disposal so before I give up on myself, I am going to try. It's important to keep a good attitude right now. I don't have to be perfect. I am allowed to make mistakes as all writers do. So, forgetting the need to immediately be an A+ student who is on my way to Harvard tomorrow, I can simply take a deep breath and begin with a sentence starter.

I'll choose, "Of course _____" because that seems easy enough. Then I ask myself, "Of course what?"

Perhaps, on a scratch sheet of paper, I can fill in the blanks for each of the three parts I want to include in this sentence.

1. A part of the conclusion restates—not repeats, but restates—the claim.

   How I can restate the claim:

   > Schools ought to make time each day for young people to relax, play, and reenergize.

2. A part of the conclusion restates—not repeats, but restates— the evidence.

   How I can restate the evidence:

   > An expert says that kids need time to just be kids.

3. A part of the conclusion cements the claim and the evidence through a direct line of logical reasoning. How I can insert one line of logical reasoning that logically connects the claim and the evidence:

   > It makes sense that schools want what's best for their students, so they'll listen to the experts.

   Now let's put everything I have together. As mentioned, I'll start with the phrase, "Of course _____ " and then start plugging stuff in.

   > Of course, it makes sense that schools want what's best for their students _____.

Hey, that's pretty good. Let's see if I can add one of the other parts in.

Of course, it makes sense that schools want what's best for their students, so when an expert says that kids need time to just be kids _____.

Very nice. I just inserted a restatement of the evidence. Let's see if I can add the last part in.

Of course, it makes sense that schools want what's best for their students, so when an expert says that kids need time to just be kids, schools ought to make time each day for young people to relax, play, and reenergize.

Wow, did I just do what I think I did? Now, read the whole short response through top to bottom to see if it works.

The school should offer students time each day to relax, play, and reenergize. Dr. Tim Marky, a child psychologist from Reynolds University, says that kids must have time to simply be kids. Of course, it makes sense that schools want what's best for their students, so when an expert says that kids need time to just be kids, schools ought to make time each day for young people to relax, play, and reenergize.

Looky there . . . I did it! Now, could I rewrite it again? Of course, nothing is ever perfect. However, let me circle back and check a few more things.

How's my spelling? How's my punctuation?

Pretty good. I think I am ready to present this short response. I made it!

Remember, for all the nuance dissected above in the Write-Aloud, all we are really doing is answering one simple question: how does the evidence support the claim?

Of course, for some students, writing such complex sentences might exceed their current capability and their conclusion will not include three parts but rather just one or two.

For example, these conclusions might be more closely aligned with the work your students produce:

▶ The school should offer students time each day to relax, play, and reenergize. Dr. Tim Marky, a child psychologist from Reynolds University, says that kids must have time to simply be kids. If schools want the best for their kids, they will listen.

▶ The school should offer students time each day to relax, play, and reenergize. Dr. Tim Marky, a child psychologist from Reynolds University, says that kids must have time to simply be kids. The evidence says kids need time for fun, so teachers should make sure that students have this.

▶ The school should offer students time each day to relax, play, and reenergize. Dr. Tim Marky, a child psychologist from Reynolds University, says that kids must have time to simply be kids. Because schools care about their students, they will listen to Dr. Tim Marky and make sure kids have a break every day.

There's nothing "wrong" with any of these examples. After all, we must remember that learning to write well happens on a continuum and it would be preposterous to presume that some of our younger writers could crank out some of the sophisticated model sentences I highlighted earlier.

Yet it's entirely reasonable to guide all students toward making sure that their Cement It! conclusion answers this question: how does the evidence support the claim? (What's the reason?)

How artfully they are able to answer will mature as they mature as writers and put in more seat time developing their craft. The more they read, the more they write, the more they practice, the higher their abilities will rise.

Finally, remember this: don't expect grand slams out of the gate. But also, don't underestimate your students' ability to learn this process.

ACTION STEP 5: Demonstrate How to Revise a Closing Statement

It's time to revise your Cement It! sentences in order to demonstrate the power of—and essential need for—revision.

OBJECTIVE: Clean up spelling and grammatical errors in our Cement It! work.

CLAIM IT!   If we paint these walls green, it will help students feel more comfortable.

CITE IT!   According to a new study, the color green ranks 19% higher than any other color choice for classroom walls because of green's connection with nature.

CEMENT IT!   Since students ~~performs~~ perform better in school when they feel most ~~cumfortable~~ comfortable, painting the ~~Classroom~~ classroom walls green makes good sense.

· · · · · ·

CLAIM IT!   Students eat too much pizza.

CITE IT!   According to Dr. Joel Hammer, kids between the ages of 8–14 are eating pizza an average of 3 times per week.

CEMENT IT!   Because experts like ~~dr.~~ Dr. Hammer believe ~~yung~~ young people need a ~~a~~ diet that includes a wide variety of foods, ~~Students~~ students should eat less pizza.

· · · · · ·

CLAIM IT!   Teachers ought to expect that parents will sometimes help their kids with homework.

CITE IT!   A new study from Chaplin College has found that 81% of parents assist with homework at least once a week.

CEMENT IT!   With research showing that this many ~~parent helps~~ parents help their children, teachers can't be ~~supersurprised~~ surprised that students sometimes get help ~~@~~ at home.

. . . . . .

CLAIM IT!   The school should offer students time each day to relax, play, and reenergize.

CITE IT!   Dr. Tim Marky, a child psychologist from Reynolds University, says that kids must have time to simply be kids.

CEMENT IT!   Of course, it makes sense that schools want what's best for ~~they're~~ their students, so when an expert says that kids need time ~~two~~ to just be kids, schools ought to make ~~tim~~ time each day for ~~Young People~~ young people to relax, play, and reenergize.

ANOTHER GREAT TIME FOR A GRAMMAR, USAGE, OR SPELLING MINI-LESSON

Yes, we took advantage of the opportunity to insert a targeted mini-lesson in the Cite It! chapter, but remember, these are young writers and the rules of spelling, grammar, and usage in English can be both confusing and extensive. This means that now might be a wonderful occasion to do a whole-class lesson that attacks one of the more persnickety issues you might notice continually bedeviling your students.

Of course, there's no right or wrong way to approach this—the teacher at the front of the room is always the one best suited to make the call on how often to mix in an interstitial lesson (a teaching opportunity that exists in the spaces between other academic objectives) as well as which standard gets selected to laser in on. In fact, it's quite reasonable to presume that the frequency and time spent on each mini-lesson might vary from classroom to classroom and grade to grade.

While comma usage, commonly confused homophones, fragments, and run-ons often present challenges for young writers, experience has proven to me that nailing down the basics of subject-verb agreement is a skill that never fails to pay big dividends for maturing writers. This means that now might be a great time to more deeply dive into why and how you revised the Cement It! sentence used in the model just provided in order to empower kids to own this core writing skill.

> *Nailing down the basics of subject-verb agreement is a skill that never fails to pay big dividends for maturing writers.*

Subject-Verb Agreement Mini-Lesson

ORIGINAL MATERIAL (only emphasizing the SVA error): Since **students performs** better in school when they feel most comfortable, painting the classroom walls green makes good sense.

REWRITTEN MATERIAL: Since **students perform** better in school when they feel most comfortable, painting the classroom walls green makes good sense.

EXPLANATION:

The **subject** is the person, place, thing, or idea that the sentence is about. In the example provided, the subject is STUDENTS.

The **verb** tells what the subject does or is. In the example provided, the verb is PERFORM.

In general, a singular subject requires a singular verb and a plural subject (plural meaning more than one person, place, thing, or idea) requires a plural verb. This is how writers make sure the subject and the verb agree with one another.

To make a subject plural, writers (usually, but not always) add an *s*.

To make a verb plural, writers normally (not always, but usually) remove the *s*.

Singular Subject	Singular Verb
girl	dances

Example: *The girl dances on the stage.*

Plural Subject	Plural Verb
girls	dance

Example: *The girls dance on the stage.*

Singular Subject	Singular Verb
dog	sits

Example: *The dog sits under the tree.*

Plural Subject	Plural Verb
dogs	sit

Example: *The dogs sit under the tree.*

Since the subject in the model sentence (STUDENTS) is plural, the verb must also be plural (PERFORM).

Plural Subject	Plural Verb
students	perform

Example: Since **students perform** better in school when they feel most comfortable, painting the classroom walls green makes good sense.

This is the simple principle behind subject-verb agreement.

ACTION STEP 6: Task Students With Revising Their Cement It! Conclusion

We are back to teacher choice on how to best assign students' next revision task. You can have students come to the front of the room and share a "before and after" for everyone to see, you can visit each of your collaborative groupings to see how kids evolved from A to B in their writing, you can encourage kids to use the frames and sentence starters provided earlier. Indeed, the possibilities are plentiful and there is no "right" or "wrong" way to approach this part of the lesson.

The only real "rules" are that ALL conclusions must:

▸ be edited for spelling, grammar, and word usage.

▸ include a clear reasoning why the evidence supports the claim.

TASK: Have students revise their Cement It! conclusions.

Hone the Three Skills of Successfully Cementing a Conclusion

As before, we'll begin first by reading and then evaluating conclusions through a set of three different lenses before tasking students with completing their own Cement It! assignments.

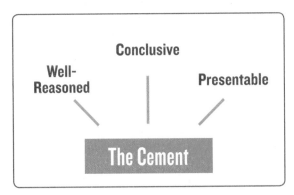

Read the following, assess the conclusion, and have students score the orange Cement It! sentence (3, 2, or 1) using the scoring guide that follows.

Making sure that schools serve their students healthy, delicious food for lunch stands out as an important issue for parents. According to research published by the National School Lunch Program, schools reported that students had eaten more fruits and vegetables, had longer attention spans, and had fewer behavior problems when they were served tasty, nutritious meal options. With the data showing that kids get many benefits from being served a healthy, delicious lunch, it makes perfect sense that parents think it's important for schools to serve these types of meals.

WELL-REASONED: In terms of how logically the evidence is connected to the claim:

> ▸ 3 points if the evidence is directly connected to the claim through a strong, sensible, and clear line of reasoning

> ▸ 2 points if the evidence is somewhat connected to the claim through a line of reasoning that is good but not great

> ▸ 1 point if the evidence is only slightly connected to the claim and only offers a small amount of good, logical reasoning

MY SCORE: _____

CONCLUSIVE: In terms of how conclusive the conclusion to their short response is, ask students to give themselves a score from 1 to 3:

> ▸ 3 points if the conclusion arrives at a definite end point for the ideas that were presented in a tone that is convincing and assertive

> ▸ 2 points if the conclusion ends the short response in a way that does deliver a closing but is not very powerful, confident, or definite

- ▸ 1 point if the conclusion doesn't do a good job of ending the short response and there's a feeling that the matter still isn't really settled

  MY SCORE: _____

PRESENTABLE: In terms of how presentable *the entire* short response is . . .

- ▸ 3 points if the claim is highly reasonable and richly expressed, the evidence is relevant, strong, and accurate, the conclusion is well reasoned and conclusive, and the entire short response is well written (i.e., nearly 100 percent free from spelling and grammatical errors)

- ▸ 2 points if the claim is somewhat reasonable, the evidence is fairly relevant and strong, the conclusion delivers a decent closing, and the entire short response is acceptably written (i.e., has a few spelling and grammatical errors that ought to have been caught in the proofreading process)

- ▸ 1 point if the claim is weak, the evidence isn't very supportive, the conclusion doesn't bring the ideas to an end point, and/or it's poorly written (i.e., has multiple spelling and grammatical errors that definitely should have been caught in the proofreading process)

  MY SCORE: _____

BONUS: Does this claim have a certain special something, that little extra piece of strength and quality that makes it deserving of a bonus point? (Add 1 point if the answer is yes.)

  BONUS POINT: _____   GRAND TOTAL: _____

Follow the same procedure with the following samples:

- ► Yellow dogs are smarter than white dogs. Three of my neighbors have yellow dogs and all of them are much more intelligent than my white dog. **Given that the evidence proves the point, it's clear which dogs are more intelligent.**

- ► Hot dogs should always be topped with either ketchup or mustard. As the author of the online article "How to Properly Eat a Hot Dog" states, "people who do not put either of these condiments on their hot dogs are making a big mistake." **Because an expert on hot dog eating said it's true, people should always use mustard or ketchup if they want to enjoy their food.**

- ► Reading about monsters is more enjoyable than reading about rabbits. Scary monsters make boys smile. **This means rabbits are not as good to read about.**

What Does It Mean to Cement a Conclusion in a Well-Reasoned Manner?

Ask 10 different students what the term "well reasoned" means and you're likely to get 10 different answers (and a couple of blank stares). It's a blue-ribbon academic phrase, one that most of your kids might not fully grasp. Therefore, be overt and be deliberate in defining the term.

Take your time with this one. Understanding what the term "well reasoned" means is not a "gimme" by any stretch of the imagination.

A well-reasoned conclusion logically and clearly explains why the evidence that has been cited supports the claim. Writers do not want to leave it to chance that audiences will "infer" why the evidence supports the claim; rock-solid writers directly connect and explain how the support they cite proves the truth of the claim that has been asserted.

Logical. Clear. Based in common sense. Well-reasoned conclusions *explain why* the evidence supports the claim.

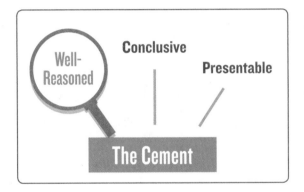

Mastering Short-Response Writing: Claim It! Cite It! Cement It! © 2016 by Alan Sitomer • Scholastic Inc. • scholastic.com/MSRWresources

Example:

Well-Reasoned Conclusion	Poorly Reasoned Conclusion
Teachers ought to expect that parents will sometimes help their kids with homework. A new study from Chaplin College has found that 81% of parents assist with homework at least once a week. Because the data shows that so many parents are already helping their children with homework, teachers would be silly not to expect that this will happen in their own class.	Teachers ought to expect that parents will sometimes help their kids with homework. A new study from Chaplin College has found that 81% of parents assist with homework at least once a week. Of course, Chaplin College is in one part of the country so that doesn't mean that kids in New York get homework help from their parents.
If we paint these walls green, it will help students feel more comfortable. According to a new study, the color green ranks 19% higher than any other color choice for classroom walls because of green's connection with nature. Since it makes sense that students will perform better in school when they feel more comfortable, painting the classroom walls green, a color that reminds people of nature, is a smart idea.	If we paint these walls green, it will help students feel more comfortable. According to a new study, the color green ranks 19% higher than any other color choice for classroom walls because of green's connection with nature. Since some kids like to be different, though, choosing a less popular color than green—like pink or blue or purple—could also be a good idea.

Ask students to make a claim, cite supportive evidence, and then cement their short response with a well-reasoned conclusion about . . .

- ▶ the best musical instrument for a young person to learn.

- ▶ the greatest gift to give to a mom on Mother's Day.

- ▶ the importance of getting a good night's sleep.

WELL-REASONED: In terms of how logically the evidence is connected to the claim:

- ▶ 3 points if the evidence is directly connected to the claim through a strong, sensible, and clear line of reasoning

- ▶ 2 points if the evidence is somewhat connected to the claim through a line of reasoning that is good but not great

- ▶ 1 point if the evidence is only slightly connected to the claim and only offers a small amount of good, logical reasoning

GATEKEEPING CHECKPOINT: Though only three examples have been provided, you might want to assign as many as 20 different tasks. Continue to assign formative practice for this area of study until you feel your students are ready to move on.

What Does It Mean to Cement a Conclusion in a Conclusive Manner?

Although this seems like a no-brainer, when it comes to student writing, conclusions are *not* automatically conclusive. In fact, if you've read enough student papers over the course of your career (as I have), you've probably read scores of conclusions that opened up more windows than they closed doors.

According to the dictionary, the word *conclusion* means "the end or close; the final part; the last main division of a discourse."

On the other hand, the word *conclusive* is an adjective that means "decisive, convincing, and serving to settle an issue or decide a question."

In other words, kids can come to the end of their short response without ever having definitively and powerfully settled the matter at hand. In short-response writing, we know how critical it is for students to concretely and convincingly close the door on their short response with a definitive concluding sentence. Therefore, we make sure young writers author conclusive conclusions.

A conclusive ending to your short response arrives at a definite end point for your ideas in a tone that is powerful, convincing, and assertive. For your conclusion to be conclusive, it has to be final, unambiguous, and clear. Readers must know where you stand and you must convey your position with certainty and authority.

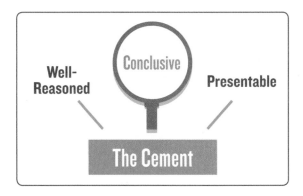

Example:

Conclusive Ending	Inconclusive Ending
It's critical that teachers send the clear message that bullying will not be tolerated at school. The U.S. Department of Health and Human Services says that students who are bullied can suffer from depression, anxiety, and low academic performance. Since the evidence proves how harmful bullying is for students, classroom teachers must make sure that bullying is not tolerated in order to do what's best for the kids and the campus.	It's critical that teachers send the clear message that bullying will not be tolerated at school. The U.S. Department of Health and Human Services says that students who are bullied can suffer from depression, anxiety, and low academic performance. Of course, there are other people like principals, librarians, and even cafeteria employees who can help, so maybe teachers want to talk about bullying with everyone who works at their school.
Serving vanilla-and-chocolate-swirl-flavored ice cream cake adds an extra dash of awesomeness to a kid's birthday party. A surprising new survey shows that 8 out of 10 kids say they have more fun at birthday parties when swirled ice cream cake is served. Because a good host always tries to think of what their guests will most enjoy, serving swirled ice cream cake is the most highly recommended dessert if you want to throw a memorable birthday party.	Serving vanilla-and-chocolate-swirl-flavored ice cream cake adds an extra dash of awesomeness to a kid's birthday party. A surprising new survey shows that 8 out of 10 kids say they have more fun at birthday parties when swirled ice cream cake is served. Because not all guests always like ice cream, a good host can also serve cookies in order to make a kid's birthday party amazing.

Ask students to make a claim, cite supportive evidence, and then cement their short response with a conclusive ending to their short response about . . .

- ▶ the best way to calm a crying baby.

- ▶ the worst way to study for a test.

- ▶ the best thing about having a day off from school.

CONCLUSIVE: In terms of how conclusive the conclusion to their short response is, ask students to give themselves a score from 1 to 3:

- ▶ 3 points if the conclusion arrives at a definite end point for the ideas that were presented in a tone that is convincing and assertive

- ▶ 2 points if the conclusion ends the short response in a way that does deliver a closing but is not very powerful, confident, or definite

- ▶ 1 point if the conclusion doesn't do a good job of ending the short response and there's a feeling that the matter still isn't really settled

GATEKEEPING CHECKPOINT: Though only three examples have been provided, you might want to assign as many as 20 different tasks. Continue to assign formative practice for this area of study until you feel your students are ready to move on.

What Does It Mean to Craft a Presentable Conclusion?

And so we arrive at the home stretch. Not only is our conclusion at the doorstep of being finalized, but our entire short response will be finished as well.

This is also the moment where we know that one very important thing still must happen before we proceed. Not only must we ensure that our conclusion is ready for prime time, but we have to make sure that our entire short response is ready to make its official debut.

That means it's time to proofread—not just the conclusion but everything we have written in our short response top to bottom.

I like to put it to young writers like this: cement seals. It's final, firm, and (practically) permanent. No one pours cement with a sense that they are going to return to their work a little bit later in order to adjust a smidgen of this or a tad of that. When you cement something, there is a commitment involved.

Our commitment is that we are through with drafting at this point; it's time to officially submit our work. A presentable short response is one that has been proofread top to bottom by its author before its final submission. It's a last read.

Spelling, grammar, punctuation, logic, rich vocabulary, clearly expressing ideas, and so on . . . nothing is off the table. If you can see a way to improve your work, you do it no matter how many times you have already read and reread and written and rewritten each of these sentences. Why? Because you know this is the final opportunity to make sure your material is in the best shape it can be.

There may be new short responses to write, but this short response is going to be officially submitted and then put in the rearview mirror of your writing life. That means that after you turn it in, there is no going back. After this final read, it's on to new horizons, so take advantage of this last opportunity to improve your efforts as best as you can and make it count.

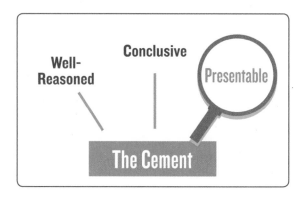

Example:

Presentable	Not Presentable
Doctors agree that eating too much candy is detrimental to a child's health. While Dr. Sarah Polley does say that some candy is okay, her expert opinion is that serving sweets ought to be rare and certainly not every day. Since there is no evidence of doctors anywhere recommending that parents serve their children lots of candy every day, it's clear that kids need to limit the amount of sweets they eat.	Doctors agree that eating to much candy is to detrimental to a child's health. While dr Sarah Polley does say that some candy is o-k her expert opinion is that serving sweets ought 2 B rare and certainly not every day. Since there is no is no evidence of doctors anywhere recommending that parents serve they're children lots of candy, they shouldn't.
Sleepover parties can be fun but usually a kid doesn't get too much sleep. This is a problem because sleep studies by the National Sleep Foundation show that young people need 60% more rest than what they normally get at overnight parties. With the research showing how much less sleep young people get at sleepover parties, kids shouldn't have them on school nights because being well rested for class is important.	Slepover parties can be fun but usually a kid doesnt get two much sleep. This a problem because sleep studes by the national sleep foundation show that young people need sixty % more rest than what they normally get @ overnight parties. With the research showing how much less sleep yung people get @ sleepover parties kids shouldnt hav them on school nights b/c being well rested for classes are important.

A Few Final Tips for Elevating Performance

READ THE RESPONSE IN ISOLATION TO MAKE SURE IT MAKES SENSE BY ITSELF

Reread only your response (without rereading the question) once you are done writing in order to make sure your response makes sense all by itself. Rock-solid short responses do NOT require the audience to have read the original writing prompt. The material needs to make sense all on its own. That means the student must have provided an answer to the question as well as created a context for the answer without requiring anyone to have an inkling about the query that triggered the reply in the first place.

For example:

ASSIGNMENT: According to the article "Parents, Watch Those Sleepovers," what concern does the author have about these types of parties for kids?

Response With Context	Response Without Context
Sleepover parties can be fun but usually a kid doesn't get too much sleep. This is a problem because sleep studies by the National Sleep Foundation show that young people need 60% more rest than what they normally get at overnight parties. With the research showing how much less sleep young people get at sleepover parties, kids shouldn't have them on school nights because being well rested for class is important.	Unfortunately, a kid doesn't get too much sleep. As they said, young people need 60% more rest than what they normally get at overnight parties. Their research shows why kids shouldn't have them on school nights.

Here is a query young writers always want to ask themselves during the "presentable" stage of short-response writing: "If I reread my reply without knowing what the question was, would my short response still make sense?"

APPLY THE THREE Cs ACROSS THE DISCIPLINES

Having students write across the disciplines is an excellent way to amplify comprehension in any subject area because short-response writing demands that students think through key concepts and demonstrate their understanding of the ideas being presented in class regardless of the curricular content being taught. Indeed, there are scores of research briefs on the benefits of "writing to learn."

In this way, short-response writing is (for the most part) not restricted to any one specific subject area. In other words, a student can just as easily make a claim, support it with strong evidence, and bring his or her short response to a well-reasoned conclusion by responding to prompts across the disciplines: from science to art to music to history to language arts, nothing is off the table. Heck, using the Three Cs can even prove to be a home run in math!

> The equilateral triangle has two features that are always alike. According to the rules of geometry, the first feature is that all three sides of the triangle must be the same length. The second characteristic is that all three of the internal angles must be exactly alike and measure 60°. If these two things can be proven true, the rules of geometry say that any triangle that meets these guidelines must be equilateral.

Writing has been proven to be one of the most effective ways to develop thinking. Once students know how to craft rock-solid short responses using the Three Cs (Claim It! Cite It! Cement it!), they have the lifelong ability to use writing as a tool to learn.

In history:

Abraham Lincoln still ranks as America's favorite president. A recent survey by the American Political Science Association says that Abraham Lincoln owns the top spot, ahead of George Washington, Franklin D. Roosevelt, and Theodore Roosevelt. Many other polls show Lincoln coming in at number one as well. Even though he's been gone for a long time now, the accomplishments of Abraham Lincoln were so significant that, according to many credible sources, he still is the most popular United States president in history.

In science:

Photosynthesis is essential for life on Earth and might be our planet's most important source of energy. The National Science Foundation says that photosynthesis supports almost all life on our planet. Since plants can make their own food by converting sunlight into energy, the rest of the planet can live off of plants. And plants sustain life at the bottom of the ocean, high on mountaintops, and everywhere in between. Since sunlight is so essential to plants, and plants are so essential to the life of all other species on Earth, the importance of photosynthesis can't be denied.

In art:

Though there have been lots of great artists, the article "Masterpieces in Art" says it's clear the greatest painter of all time was Leonardo da Vinci. As the texts points out, da Vinci painted the *Mona Lisa*, the most famous painting in history, *The Last Supper*, the most famous religious painting in history, and the ceiling of the Sistine Chapel, one of the most visited tourist destinations in history. Because no other painter has created nearly as many masterpieces, the author's claim that Leonardo da Vinci is the greatest painter of all time is well supported and makes good sense.

 Mastering Short-Response Writing: Claim It! Cite It! Cement It! © 2016 by Alan Sitomer • Scholastic Inc. • scholastic.com/MSRWresources

MOVE YOUR STUDENTS AWAY FROM COLOR-CODING ON YOUR OWN SCHEDULE

The best person to decide when to have young writers move away from color-coding their short responses (our system of using blue, green, and orange) and into writing short responses top-to-bottom in one color is the teacher at the front of the room.

There's no rush. There's no exact science about when to make that decision. At some point, yes, you'll want your students to write their responses in just one color, but when this modification happens is up to you.

How will you know when they're ready? When do you take the training wheels off of the bike? Trust your gut, you'll know.

VIEW REBUTTALS, COUNTERCLAIMS, WARRANTS, AND REFUTATIONS AS NEXT-LEVEL AIMS

Admittedly, short-response writing, particularly argumentative writing, can include more wrinkles and nuances than those we've covered in this text. Writers can include rebuttals, counterclaims, warrants, refutations, qualifiers, and more.

All of the above are "next-level" aims. The Three Cs are all about locking in the core fundamentals of short-response writing. Put another way, teaching young writers how to make counterclaims before they can simply make claims—rock-solid ones—is putting the cart before the horse.

By all means, if your students are ready to advance to more sophisticated levels of composing short responses, roar ahead. However, if they have not yet mastered the fundamental skills illuminated herein, our belief is that it's better to lock down the basics before moving forward.

Moving On (Or Rather, Going Forward)

Having the ability to write rock-solid short responses is a skill students will need for, well . . . the foreseeable future. Decades, at least. High school, college, grad school, the work force—the thinking skills the Three Cs help to develop will always have tremendous value.

That means that we've arrived at a place where students now know how to cement their conclusions, but we have not arrived at a finish line. As your young writers mature, their vocabulary will expand, their ability to express ideas in a more sophisticated manner will grow, and the content and the complexity of the work they generate will deepen.

Do you need to circle back for additional fine-tuning of editorial skills? Perhaps. Do you need to bring in more rigorous source text that demands students wrestle with higher-level challenges? Maybe.

The beauty and the bane of the craft of writing is that no one ever perfects it. There are always higher mountains to climb and deeper oceans to plumb. Yet when you take a look at where your kids once were and where they are now, I hope you take a moment to give yourself a big, fat "CONGRATS!"

Measurable growth ought now be in hand and none of it was given; you earned it.

Cheers to you.

CHAPTER 7

Providing Productive and Positive Feedback

Take a look at the following student's short response shown on page 134. What's the first thing you see?

For most of us, we can't help but register all the errors. The things that are wrong with the writing leap out at us. Our attention is almost automatically drawn to the misspelled words, the capitalization errors, the nonindented paragraph, and so on. The piece shows promise but the poor execution steals our eyes.

The beauty and the bane of the craft of writing is that no one ever perfects it. There are always higher mountains to climb and deeper oceans to plumb.

Rights for Chimps
by Jacqueline Adams

Last December, an animal rights group filed lawsuits on behalf of four chimpanzees in New York State. The Nonhuman Rights Project wants the chimps—two pets and two research subjects—to be considered legal persons, which would make it illegal to keep them in captivity. Judges denied each of the petitions, but lawyers plan to fight the decision.

The group argues that chimpanzees' advanced cognitive abilities make them very similar to humans, so it's unfair to keep them in captivity or use them for biomedical experiments. Opponents argue that chimps are vital for scientific research such as vaccine development.

Nearly 2,000 chimpanzees live in the U.S., many alone in small cages. Stephen Ross, a primatologist at Lincoln Park Zoo in Chicago, thinks chimps should be housed in an appropriate environment with other chimps, but thinks that the lawsuits may go too far. "The goal is to improve living conditions for chimpanzees," Ross says. "The question is whether seeking personhood is the right way to go about that."

Student Name: Jake

Task: Explain why the lawyers from the Nonhuman Rights Project believe chimpanzees deserve to be considered legal persons.

The lawyers frome the nunhuman right project belive its Unfair to keep chimps in captivity. They say it's not right to Use them for biomedical experiments and they also said chimps are like persosns. Since no chimpanzee wants to live in a small cage the lawyers field a lawsuit in New York State.

Now take a look at the same student's short-response writing sample from a few weeks earlier (using the same source text and prompt).

Rights for Chimps
by Jacqueline Adams

Last December, an animal rights group filed lawsuits on behalf of four chimpanzees in New York State. The Nonhuman Rights Project wants the chimps—two pets and two research subjects—to be considered legal persons, which would make it illegal to keep them in captivity. Judges denied each of the petitions, but lawyers plan to fight the decision.

The group argues that chimpanzees' advanced cognitive abilities make them very similar to humans, so it's unfair to keep them in captivity or use them for biomedical experiments. Opponents argue that chimps are vital for scientific research such as vaccine development.

Nearly 2,000 chimpanzees live in the U.S., many alone in small cages. Stephen Ross, a primatologist at Lincoln Park Zoo in Chicago, thinks chimps should be housed in an appropriate environment with other chimps, but thinks that the lawsuits may go too far. "The goal is to improve living conditions for chimpanzees," Ross says. "The question is whether seeking personhood is the right way to go about that."

Student Name: Jake

Task: Explain why the lawyers from the Nonhuman Rights Project believe chimpanzees deserve to be considered legal persons.

Because it's so unfair to keep them in captivity or use them for biomedical experiments.

What do you notice between the two samples? That's right, a lot of growth on the part of that student, in many critical areas. The spelling and grammar may be correct in the first sample, but the message is so much richer in the second.

Now take the following into consideration. Four months prior to writing these samples, Jake's mother passed away from pancreatic cancer. She was a single mom, too, so Jake and his younger sister now live with an uncle he hardly knew prior to his mother's passing. Although Jake has not yet made any new, close friends at his new school, he will because he's a good kid, one who is especially diligent about looking after his younger sister, especially when she starts to cry about how she misses her mommy. Of course, sometimes Jake still walks into the room with a look in his eyes like he's waiting for someone to wake him up from some horrible nightmare, but his new teacher is working hard to help him transition positively into a new life.

"Teach the writer, not the writing," is a motto worth its weight in gold.

What happens when you consider Jake's work a third time, knowing this new information about him? Instead of seeing the errors in the writing, you probably see the humanity of the writer.

"Teach the writer, not the writing," is a motto worth its weight in gold. The way this is done is by becoming adept at providing high-quality feedback that serves the person doing the work as opposed to providing (mostly error-based) observations about the work that has been done.

When we see only a writing sample, we see what amounts to a mere snapshot of a student's abilities. And then we gravitate— whether consciously or unconsciously—toward identifying what's wrong with the piece. When we see the second writing sample side-by-side with the first, we get to see the student's work within a context. We have valuable insights. But when we learn about the whole child, the real kid who is sitting in that chair, the path by which we can best elevate his or her abilities reveals itself. This is where the art of teaching meets the science of teaching.

The 2 + 1 + 1 Principle of Productive, Purposeful Feedback

Feedback is so important if we want students to make meaningful gains. And getting great at providing productive and positive feedback is a skill that will move mountains in terms of elevating performance. Thus, the 2 + 1 + 1 principle of providing feedback to your young writers.

THE "2": STARTING WITH TWO POSITIVE COMMENTS

When you start providing feedback to your students' short-response writing, note two positive things the student did well. There are several reasons why this is a good idea.

Seeing the merits in student work before seeing the shortfalls is simply good practice. When you begin by acknowledging what's right about the work, the writer feels validated, encouraged, and respected. If you start with what's wrong, however, a kid's defenses go up, not to mention their insecurities: "I stink, I'm no good, I can't write, I'm stupid." When people heap praise on us, our ears open. When people offer condemnation, we close ourselves off. That's the human way. As the old saying goes, you catch more flies with honey than you do vinegar.

Furthermore, when you point out the things students are doing well, it reinforces the correctly executed skills. It inspires young writers to continue to do more of what they've just properly done.

Be overt and be effusive. When a student writer does something well, make sure you let him or her know. And yes, there will always be a minimum of two things you can find to praise. It all depends on the eyes through which you choose to see your students' efforts.

TARGETING ONE SKILL FOR IMPROVEMENT (THE FIRST "1" IN 2 + 1 + 1)

After finding two positives, select just one skill requiring attention at first—even if there are many, many more. Pointing out every single "problem" and then suggesting how each one can be solved often causes young writers lots of anxiety. It's hard enough to hear you made one blunder, but hearing you made eight in only three sentences can be downright devastating.

TARGETING ONE MORE SKILL FOR IMPROVEMENT (THE SECOND "1" IN 2 + 1 + 1)

Too much feedback overwhelms students, plain and simple. After all, any kid who is learning to write well is going to make mistakes but no kid is going to learn how to fix five mistakes all at once. Each of us only has so much cognitive bandwidth. This means your feedback MUST take the student's capacity to absorb your commentary into consideration. Design your feedback to attend to what's most important (in your opinion) while remaining cognizant of the fact that young writers only have the ability to attend to a limited amount of information at any one time.

Too much feedback overwhelms students, plain and simple. Design your feedback to attend to what's most important while remaining cognizant of the fact that young writers only have the ability to attend to a limited amount of information at any one time.

After students have addressed one area, you might decide to zero in on one more thing. Perhaps you want to zero in on how to properly use quotation marks when citing evidence from a text and also do a second micro-lesson on *it's* versus *its* even if it is a concept you have covered multiple times before. When you're on the front lines of teaching students how to write, it's simply not possible to allow everything to always slide. *Mastering Short-Response Writing* is, after all, designed first and foremost to be user-friendly for educators and we all know there comes a point when a teacher of writing just has to take a stand.

Just be wary of going too far too soon. Reaching to hit a third correction and then a fourth might be highly tempting, yet don't forget, many a kid has mastered the "Yep, I got this" head nod while inside their brain the only thought they are able to follow is, "I sure hope there's pizza for lunch."

> ▶ **Do** purposefully tackle critical writing standards.
>
> ▶ **Don't** try to stuff 10 pounds' worth of knowledge into a 5-pound bag.

The Fallacy of Dense Epidermis

Don't teach your students to "develop a thicker skin"; teach your students that "your significance as a person has absolutely zero to do with the writing you produce."

Strong writing teachers understand how to get the message across that their students are whole, valued, and deserving of respect regardless of whether they know how to do things like properly cite textual evidence in an expository short response.

Remember, receiving feedback that doesn't take the writer's feelings into consideration can too easily induce embarrassment and shame—especially for students who are not quite yet wielding words like Toni Morrison.

"You are not your work." It's a lesson that students are well served to learn. (And you'd be hard pressed to find a professional author who's been spared from learning that lesson either. Usually the hard way.)

"You are not your work." It's a lesson that students are well served to learn.

If on the one hand teachers have to realize that their students' feelings do matter, and that their feedback *must* take this into consideration, then on the other hand students *must* realize that their sense of self-worth cannot be tied to the writing they produce.

Taking a chronically positive bent is not soft or fluff, it's simply smart instructional practice.

Productive and Positive Feedback Exemplified

LEXI

Here's a short-response written by Lexi. What follows is a Think-Aloud of the feedback she was given.

Bunny Hop
by Charlye Dehort

Rabbits these days sure are competitive! Last year, Switzerland hosted the first European Rabbit Hopping Championships. Bunnies in the competition bounce through an obstacle course earning points for speed and how high they jump.

Paula Watkins, manager of the Cape Fear House Rabbit Society in North Carolina, says, "[Rabbits] need a lot of exercise and stimulation, and they like to run around." She stresses, however, that training must be done humanely.

Rabbits have strong hind-leg muscles that allow some species to jump more than 1 meter (3 feet) high. If rabbits are always kept in cages, their powerful leg muscles will *atrophy*, or waste away.

Student Name: Lexi

Task: Based on the article BUNNY HOP, explain why the European Rabbit Hopping Championships can be considered beneficial for rabbits.

It can be beneficial for rabbits because it can give them more exersize, and if they get more attention they will get to be even more popular! Rabbits need all the attention they can get so they don't become extinct extinct like other animals. If we can save rabbits we can save the world.

The First Positive Comment

"Lexi, great job of starting out by actually making a go at answering the question that was asked. So many students have their work fall short because they don't begin by trying to answer what the prompt asked them to. Keep that up. Always! In math, in history . . . you'll see it over and over again. In this piece, it's clear you read the question and set out to answer it. Nice."

The Second Positive Comment

"Also, Lexi, there's a lot of growth in your attention to spelling. It wasn't that long ago that you were misspelling words that you knew how to spell, but now, I see how you are taking your time and paying more attention to the details. *Beneficial* is spelled correctly—not an easy word—*rabbits* has two *b*'s and one *t*—you got that right—and *attention* is also spelled correctly. As we've talked about, getting rid of lazy spelling habits can do a world of good for your work. Well done, your work is paying off."

Identifying Areas of Improvement

Now it's decision time. What is going to be the first area of focus you want Lexi to laser in on? In no particular order, you could choose from any one of the following:

- *Exercize* is spelled with a *z*.
- "It can be beneficial . . ." What "it" is the writer referring to?
- The second half of Lexi's claim, where she creates an argument about the popularity of rabbits preventing their extinction, is highly suspect.

And so on . . .

The big thing you must ask yourself is, "What core area of focus is going to provide the most bang for my buck right now?" In the case of Lexi, the feedback addressed the second C.

"Lexi, Triple C writing is about 1) Claim It! 2) Cite It!, and 3) Cement it! When we Cite It! what are we citing?"

Lexi is given a moment to reread her work. A light clearly goes on for her. It's evident she can see her own path to how to improve this critical part of her short response. As the teacher, you do not want to do the work for Lexi and rewrite the Cite It! sentence for her; you want her to do the work. Thus, a simple question is posed.

"Lexi, do you understand what it means to cite evidence from the text to support your claim?"

"Uh-huh."

"Do you have a new idea in mind as to how you can improve your work in this area?"

"Yep."

"Great, I'll be looking for that in your rewrite."

More could be said but this is not a scripted conversation. Since you're teaching the writer and not the writing and Lexi has given enough signals to let you know that she now knows how to improve her work, you can let Lexi run with it. No need to overteach. You can move to another area of improvement.

That unclear pronoun reference in Lexi's claim is not only something that is easily remedied but it's also something that frequently bedevils developing writers.

"Hey, Lexi, if I said to you, 'There is no doubt, it is going to be very negative for mice,' what question would you ask yourself?"

Lexi thinks about it for a moment. "Um, what is going to be very negative for mice?"

"Exactly! Because you do not know what the "it" refers to. But if I said, 'The fact that there is no more cheese left in the city is going to be very negative for mice,' then you know what I am talking about, correct? Now pretend you had not read the short passage about the Bunny Hop and instead read only your answer."

Lexi listens as her claim is read aloud to her.

She gets "it" (no pun intended) right away.

"Go take one more pass at this and really rock it, okay?"

"Okay."

As Lexi heads back to her desk, there's an opportunity to sneak one more thing in. Something that was noticed as a "whole-class issue" so the whole class gets addressed—but Lexi is clearly a prime target and she knows it as she walks back to her seat to do her rewrite.

"And let's everyone try to remember that when words are spelled properly for you in the reading passage—words like *exercise* with an *s* and not a *z*—it's really hard to find a reason why they are not spelled properly in your short responses."

Lexi smiles and keeps walking. Point made.

Ten minutes later, Lexi turned in the following.

Student Name: Lexi

Task: Based on the article BUNNY HOP, explain why the European Rabbit Hopping Championships can be considered beneficial for rabbits.

The European Rabbit Hopping Championships are beneficial for rabbits because it gives them lots of exercise. The text evidence states that rabbits need a lot of exercise and stimulation, and these Trials can help them do that. More exercise is good for rabbits, after eating all those carrots, they could use it.

By keeping the timeline short between when you gave Lexi feedback and when she did her revision, it's clear that the conference was a success.

ANNA

Where do you even begin when you get something like this?

Bunny Hop
by Charlye Dehort

Rabbits these days sure are competitive! Last year, Switzerland hosted the first European Rabbit Hopping Championships. Bunnies in the competition bounce through an obstacle course earning points for speed and how high they jump.

Paula Watkins, manager of the Cape Fear House Rabbit Society in North Carolina, says, "[Rabbits] need a lot of exercise and stimulation, and they like to run around." She stresses, however, that training must be done humanely.

Rabbits have strong hind-leg muscles that allow some species to jump more than 1 meter (3 feet) high. If rabbits are always kept in cages, their powerful leg muscles will *atrophy*, or waste away.

Student Name: _Anna_

Task: Based on the article BUNNY HOP, explain why the European Rabbit Hopping Championships can be considered beneficial for rabbits.

Competitions, They are good because Paula Whtkins thinks that rabbits need exersize. Why it is true is because bunnies do need to stay on a go like a human does something at 2 years old and stops for 8 years they will forget how to to do that thing. People can start something at 2 years old and finish at 3. They will probly forget evrithing at age 10. Thats 7 years. My point is you and animals auto stay on track with what they do and bunnies just can't stop.

Competions are good because you work out.

"Bunny Hop" by Charlye Dehart from *Science World* magazine, February 13, 2012.
Copyright © 2012 by Scholastic Inc. All rights reserved.

Return to the core premise of providing strong feedback: teach the writer, not the writing. And a close look at the writing reveals a great deal about the writer.

Basically, Anna got caught in the weeds early on in her work and things just snowballed from there. And who hasn't been there? The response got off to a shaky start, there was another misstep, one more fumble, and then BOOM!

Happens to the best of us. But you should still start your feedback by pointing out two positive things.

The First Positive Comment

Anna knows long before she even sits down for feedback that she blew it. There's a look of sadness in her eyes—almost shame. Noting something positive is essential for Anna right now.

But we don't want to be disingenuous. Kids can smell a fake a mile away. This means we have to look hard at the writing and find something genuinely worth appreciating.

A close read of Anna's work reveals a great deal.

"Anna, it's clear that something went haywire with this short response but I absolutely love the fact that you continued to battle and try and work the whole way through. Sure, this may be a bit of a mess but that's because you didn't give up. Let's forget about what this paper looks like right now and instead take a moment to appreciate that when times got tough, you kept going and kept making an effort. That's a big part of being successful in writing and in life. Sometimes, things go kablooey. For all of us. No one is mad at you, no one is disappointed, at some point we all spill the milk, if you know what I am saying."

Anna practically has tears in her eyes because instead of being shamed for her lack of skills she was praised for her work ethic. (Teach the writer, not the writing.)

The Second Positive Comment

"And you know what else I like is that it's clear you proofread your work. When I see your claim, I notice that you had a capital *T* in the word *They* but then it seems you changed it to a lowercase *t* because you realized that the reader has no idea who "they" are . . . so you went back in and tried to fix it by adding something about *compotions*. And of course, you ran out of room and your fix didn't really work so well but you clearly did do some proofreading before you turned it in. Overall, keep that up. Proofreading will pay off in the future a lot as you continue to improve."

The First Area of Improvement

Anna is capable of so much more. She's done work in the past that exceeds this sample by leaps and bounds, so be sure to apply the feedback with a deft, light touch.

"Anna, if you recall, we're working on our Triple C Writing. That means Claim It! Cite It! Cement It! Do you have any questions or do you just want to take another pass at this and rewrite the whole thing top to bottom on a clean sheet of paper?"

"Rewrite it all."

"Perfect. Here's a new sheet of paper."

With so much to address, simply reminding Anna of the structure and the aim of her work felt like a good enough start.

THE SECOND AREA OF IMPROVEMENT

Before Anna heads off, though, anchoring one hard skill feels like a good idea.

"Hey Anna, just one thing before you begin again. I really want you to concentrate on making a solid claim, okay? Think about it before you begin writing. Know what you want to say. That means answering the question that has been asked and then responding to the question directly. Even if the whole thing goes kablooey the second time, that's okay, but let's see if we can't get the short response started on a nice, high-quality note. Spelling, punctuation, a clear position . . . all the things we talked about. That seem like a good plan?"

"Yes."

"Any questions about how to make a claim?"

"Not really."

"Okay. Keep your chin up and go take another stab at it."

Ten minutes later, Anna turned in the following.

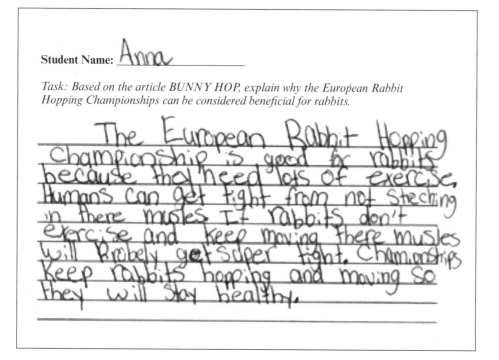

Student Name: Anna

Task: Based on the article BUNNY HOP, explain why the European Rabbit Hopping Championships can be considered beneficial for rabbits.

The European Rabbit Hopping Championship is good for rabbits because they need lots of exercise. Humans can get tight from not streching in there musles If rabbits don't exercise and keep moving there musles will probely get super tight. Championships keep rabbits hopping and moving so they will stay healthy.

Wow, right?

Of course, in the case of Anna, the first writing sample was an anomaly. Anna didn't just learn how to compose like this in 10 minutes; that's simply not possible. Anna always had some decent skills. She just tanked it on her first try . . . nothing more than that. As a result, Anna ended up discovering a hard truth about learning how to write well. She learned that at some point all writers fall flat on their face and that picking yourself up and dusting yourself off without allowing your spirit to be crushed by your "spilled milk" attempt is just part of the process.

No shame. No apologies. Just keep moving forward.

Of course, you may have wanted to drive home the same lesson to Anna that you did to Lexi (regarding the citation of textual evidence) but alas, that opportunity did not present itself with this activity. Such is life on the front lines of writing instruction. Over time, however, all challenges will have a chance to be addressed.

Three Questions Writing Teachers Must Ask Themselves

In order to set your students up for success, you are going to have to set yourself up for success. Here are three great questions to ask yourself before assigning any writing tasks.

1. Can I provide timely feedback?

2. Can I manage the paper load if I assign this task right now?

3. What's the rewrite plan?

Do not assign work until you know the answers to these questions. I had to learn this lesson the hard way. Back when I was a student, the only feedback on papers I wrote that held any value for me was my grade because it allowed me to see where I stood in terms of passing the class— the rest was just a lot of red scribbles that I didn't pay much attention to. Then I became a teacher and vowed I'd never partake in this folly.

Halfway through my first year as a rookie teacher, my name was Mr. Folly. I was spending *hours* evaluating papers that took me forever to get through and by the time I handed them back to my students— sometimes more than a week later—they'd barely remembered a darn word they'd scribbled.

My cherished feedback, so thoughtful and extensive, proved to be nothing more than a giant waste of time. They barely read it, they certainly didn't absorb it, and the only thing amplified by my efforts was my resentment toward the whole idea of trying to teach my students how to write well.

Talk about a negative feedback loop.

Avoid learning this lesson the hard way. Strong writing instructors understand that timely feedback is essential if your responses are going to have real value. However, for most teachers of writing, this presents a conundrum.

Assessing writing in general can suck up lots of time. And when you're a classroom teacher, time is a rare and precious commodity. Therefore, you face the double bind of either staying up till 1:00 in the morning just to get your students' work evaluated or providing feedback to your young writers so many days after they've composed their work that both the assignment and their response are long since forgotten.

Hmm . . . what to do?

Well, the good news is that it's not an either/or scenario. You can have your cake and eat it, too. However, first and foremost you must have a plan.

That's worth repeating: always have a plan! Below are 10 tips that can help you provide timely feedback, manage the paper load, and execute a productive rewrite plan.

Ten Tips for Providing Feedback

Here are 10 tips that can help you provide timely feedback, manage the paper load, and execute a productive plan for student revisions.

1. **Assign one short-response writing task a day for five days, starting on Monday.** On Friday, have your students revise and proofread their BEST piece of work and turn in only that one for credit (with an emphasis on "this one is REALLY going to count!").

Then on Monday, provide feedback. The students wrote for five days (lots of formative practice), yet you only had to read one assignment (a reasonable volume for the teacher), and you've gotten to see their "best" effort. Of course, this also lets you clearly see your students' strengths and weaknesses in a way that allows you to better plan your next phase of instruction.

2. **Consider the complexity of the task.** New concepts that are intellectually demanding (such as the Third C: Cement It!) almost always require on-the-spot feedback. Therefore, plan accordingly because the immediacy of feedback is essential to effective instruction. On the other hand, things like spelling mistakes don't require you to be standing over the shoulder of a student.

3. **Put yourself on a timer.** Two minutes per student paper. Set your phone's buzzer and go. You have only so much time in your day and it's not cheating your students to set firm boundaries around assessment. Get in, get out, and make sure you get feedback to students within 24 hours at the latest, not 72. For the weightier summative assessments, the rules can change, but for formative practice, maintain healthy boundaries.

4. **State what students must produce and how it will be assessed.** Evaluate your targets and let other items go. To deviate from this strategy is tempting ("I'll just correct a few dangling modifiers") but it's also like the proverbial sirens from Greek mythology calling sailors to the rocks. Be warned, this is where ships crash. Don't take the bait.

5. **Abide by your schedule in a committed, disciplined manner.** Make Facebook wait. Put *People* magazine down. Forget checking in with TMZ about the latest celebrity hook-ups. (Okay, so maybe my guilty pleasures aren't yours.)

6. **Only ask for revisions that will receive your full attention.** When students expect that their teacher will respond to their work and a response never comes, they feel diminished and unimportant. They ask themselves, "Why bother to try my best when she's not even going to read it?" If you ask for a revision, plan to weigh in on it. If you do not have time to manage the paper load of rewrites, don't ask for them.

7. **Avoid cryptic commentary.** Writing *awk* (for awkward) in the side column of a student's paper does little more than express your dissatisfaction with their work. With novice writers, comments like these often cause confusion because 1) the writer isn't always sure what exactly is *awk* about the work and 2) the writer is even less sure about how to make the work un-*awk*. Productive, positive feedback isn't about identifying what's not working; it's about offering clear, precise guidance on how to improve.

8. **Avoid platitudes.** It's common for teachers to scrawl "AWESOME!" across the top of a paper, but while we applaud the spirit of the comment, the writer is left to guess what exactly was "AWESOME!" about their work. Be precise in order to anchor skills. Instead of "AWESOME!" perhaps you write "AWESOME USE OF QUOTATION MARKS!" It takes a wee bit longer to pen but the positive returns on the extra effort make a huge difference.

9. **Provide equal time to *all* kids.** All too often low-performing students get more attention than high-performing students. Is your allocation of feedback evenly balanced across your entire classroom? Do your top writers get an equal share of your attention? Always something to keep an eye on.

10. **Plan more face-to-face time than face-to-page time.** Spending more time with your students' writing than with your student writers is an easy trap to fall into. When you make comments on

the writing, compose them as if the student were sitting right there next to you. Visualizing the student in this way as you assess written work helps keep you in sync with teaching the writer and not the writing.

Consider the Three-Day Feedback Loop

In *Results Now* (2006), Mike Schmoker writes about the detrimental effects that providing feedback can have on both a teacher and a student if a smart plan is not well in hand at the onset. Students can become confused and demoralized. Here's a mini-pacing plan that might work well for you.

Day 1	Day 2	Day 3
During the school day, have students write. On your own time, provide written feedback.	Give the written feedback to students and have them revise. On your own time, evaluate the revisions.	Confer face-to-face with students (individually or in small groups). After conferring, plot the next best path forward. Schedule a new loop according to where you are in your school year.

Help to Destigmatize Your Students

Why do we even call them struggling writers? Is there any other kind? To write well requires effort. The "better" the writing, the more effort you can presume the writer exerted. There's a direct corollary between quality work and intellectual elbow grease.

Struggle isn't just par for the course; it is the course! Students have to be delabeled. All of them are struggling writers. Even your top performers. (Maybe especially your top performers.) Writing well requires work, whether it's expository short-response or long-form narrative. There are simply no short cuts around "struggle"; it's baked into the DNA of the road all writers must walk.

> If the English language made any sense, *lackadaisical* would have something to do with a shortage of flowers.
>
> **—DOUG LARSON**

English is a cuckoo language with counterintuitive rules that can turn PhDs into thumb-suckers and construction workers into poets. Keen advice for success is everywhere and nowhere at the same time.

> Never, ever use repetitive redundancies. Don't use no double negatives. Proofread carefully to see if you any words out.
>
> **—WILLIAM SAFIRE**

Look, if you made it this far through this book, I must have earned your trust to one degree or another. Maybe it was engendered through a combination of my experience as a writer, my experience as a teacher of writing, and my washboard abs.

Okay, I have donut abs but you get the point: credibility matters. Have I walked a mile in your moccasins? Have I been placed in similar quandaries? Have I struggled to attain success in a similar way that you may have struggled?

It's because I have built a connection with you through anecdotes, empathy, experience, and so on, that you have vested your belief in me belief in me and opened up to my suggestions. And if I have not built a strong enough connection with you, it's doubtful that you are going to buy into the ideas I am offering.

Why do your students "trust" you? Have you written? Have you struggled, failed, or entirely laid an egg as a writer? Have you ever been embarrassed or confused or shamed for your lack of ability to string coherent, concise sentences together?

Have you ever read something you've written and said to yourself, "Wow, I really stink"?

If you are going to give feedback, you have to position yourself as a person who has some street cred. They say the best rehab counselors are former drug addicts. That's a not-so-polished way of saying that you have to make your own struggles with writing public for your students. If you don't, your students are apt to view you as a magician who knows all the crafty ways to continually pull all the right rabbits out of all the right hats at all the right times.

Your students are not struggling writers; they're developing writers. Frame your feedback for them accordingly. Let them know you empathize with how vulnerable they are by allowing them to know how vulnerable you are (and have been) when you write.

Writing well requires struggle, but together, teacher and student, side by side, many gains can be had.

Open a World of Possible

Carol Dweck's book *Mindsets* knocked it out of the park. A national bestseller, it became a very popular read in education circles. It's no understatement to say that Dweck's popular TED talk and her research, out of Stanford University, shifted some long-held paradigms regarding how schools ought to best teach kids.

In her work, Dweck explains why "fixed mindsets" limit achievement whereas "growth mindsets" enable people to reach lofty goals. "In a fixed mindset," she wrote, "people believe their basic qualities, like their intelligence or talent, are simply fixed traits. In a growth mindset, people believe that their most basic abilities can be developed." (Dweck, 2007)

Dweck's essential premise is that the mindset with which we approach our tasks plays a huge role—maybe a larger role than any other factor—as to whether or not people eventually attain success. In other words, what you believe about your ability to learn directly impacts whether you attain success when it comes to undertaking new and/or difficult challenges.

Consider me a big fan of Dweck's ideas. Of course, I'm a person who has engineered an entire career around advocating for the significance of engagement. For years, I've spoken and written about the value of autonomy, passion, and meaningfulness as they relate to efficacious instruction. Yet I've also always been a firm believer that the sizzle cannot come at the expense of the steak. If we are going to be successful teachers of writing, we must realize that sometimes it's okay to let kids drift away in a field of imaginative concert halls and write free-form hip-hop rap flows that paraphrase Orwellian dystopia, but other times it is entirely appropriate to make sure every student in class marches single file and properly uses an apostrophe in a grammatically correct sentence!

Bring On the Skills

Student engagement leads to a positive launch. With motivated scholars ready to seize the day, the ship of learning sets sail to sea with the wind at its back and, if the momentum continues, an outlook of blue skies and calm oceans ahead can certainly follow. Awakening passion, elevating grit, encouraging creativity, connecting to meaningfulness, and so on, are essential. And so, too, as Dweck would agree, is the hard work of building demonstrable skills.

Sadly, all the joy, verve, and dynamic instruction in the world are not going to circumvent this truism. Learning how to write well requires labor and diligent effort to build writing muscle. Toil cannot be sidestepped! Students who become excellent writers must first gain strong fluency with the fundamentals of the craft. In this regard, writing is very much like almost every other endeavor.

Beethoven, Shakespeare, Michael Jordan, Frank Lloyd Wright, Pavarotti, and zillions of other superstars in their chosen field all mastered the fundamentals of their discipline before ascending to great heights. Perhaps no one illustrates this better than Pablo Picasso. Hanging on

Mastering Short-Response Writing: Claim It! Cite It! Cement It! © 2016 by Alan Sitomer • Scholastic Inc. • scholastic.com/MSRWresources

the wall at the Museo Picasso in Barcelona, Spain, are paintings Picasso painted as a teenager, in traditional, naturalistic styles that rivaled the Old Masters. The young man's skills were far beyond his years but interestingly, the paintings gave no indication of the avant-garde artistic movements that he would champion as an adult.

It can be reasonably argued that at some point during his teenage years, Picasso had gained mastery over the fundamentals of painting. It was this early mastery that allowed him to then move beyond the boundaries of his previous work and create something so utterly unique.

Make no mistake, strong foundations and solid fundamentals are essential for brilliance to blossom. Brevity requires intellectual discipline. This is why teaching young writers how to write rock-solid short responses is so valuable: the critical thinking necessitated by mastering this skill builds brain power. Knowing how to cite, claim, and cement rock-solid short-response writing helps all children open a world of possible.

Sending you many wishes for good fortune—and good grammar!

References

Anderson, J. (2011). *10 things every writer needs to know.* Portland, ME: Stenhouse Publishers.

Archer, A. & C. A. Hughes. (2010). *Explicit instruction: Effective and efficient teaching.* New York: The Guilford Press.

Brown, H. D. (2006). *Principles of language learning and teaching.* Boston: Pearson Education, Inc.

Campbell, J. (2008). *The hero with a thousand faces: The collected works of Joseph Campbell, third edition.* Novato, CA: New World Library.

Dweck, C. S. (2006). *Mindset: The new psychology of success.* New York: Random House.

Dweck, C. S. (2015). "Carol Dweck revisits the growth mindset." *Education Week*, September 22.

Fletcher, R. (2011). *Mentor author, mentor texts: Short texts, craft notes, and practical classroom uses.* Portsmouth, NH: Heinemann.

Leograndis, D. (2006). *Fluent writing: How to teach the art of pacing.* Portsmouth, NH: Heinemann.

Oczkus, L. (2007). *Guided writing: Practical lessons, powerful results.* Portsmouth, NH: Heinemann.

The Purdue Writing Lab. https://owl.english.purdue.edu/owl/resource/588/01/

Routman, R. (2014). *Read, write, lead: Breakthrough strategies for schoolwide literacy success.* Alexandria, VA: Association for Supervision & Curriculum Development.

Tantillo, L. (2012). *The literacy cookbook: A practical guide to effective reading, writing, speaking, and listening instruction.* San Francisco: Jossey-Bass.

Index